Ron Santo
A Perfect 10

Pat Hughes
and
Rich Wolfe

Published by Lone Wolfe Press, a division of Richcraft. Distribution, marketing, publicity, interviews, and book signings handled by Wolfegang Marketing Systems, Ltd.—But Not Very.

Photo Credits:

> Courtesy of *This Old Cub,* the Santo Family, Janell Hughes, Steve Green
>
> Pages 16, 229 photos courtesy of WGN Radio, photos by Randy Lee Belice
>
> Page 120 photo courtesy of Jon Soo, Los Angeles Dodgers
>
> Page 138 photo courtesy of the *Chicago Tribune*
>
> Pages156, 159, 162 photos courtesy of Bob Vorwald
>
> Page 190 photo courtesy of the Chicago Blackhawks
>
> Page 183 photo courtesy of Scott Paulus, Milwaukee Brewers

Layout: The Printed Page, Phoenix, AZ
Cover Design: Dick Fox
Author's agent: T. Roy Gaul

Rich Wolfe can be reached at 602-738-5889

ISBN: 978-0-9846278-2-0

PAGE TWO. In 1941, the news director at a small radio station in Kalamazoo, Michigan hired Harry Caray who had been employed at a station in Joliet, Illinois. The news director's name was Paul Harvey. Yes, that PAUL HARVEY! "And now, you have the rest of the story . . . .

CHAT ROOMS

ACKNOWLEDGMENTS

Wonderful people helped make this book a reality, starting with the incredible Ellen Brewer in Edmond, Oklahoma and Lisa Liddy at The Printed Page in Phoenix—wonder women who have been indispensible sidekicks for many years. A big thanks to Cathy Gleason in Phoenix, Loras McClimon at Hohokam Park in Mesa, Jack Marlowe, the best sportswriter in Iowa and the king of Maquoketa, and to Mike Croke and Jeff Chism, the honchos at the Marriott SpringHill Suites in Lincolnshire...and, how about Mike Pruyn in Naperville, Joe Hutchison in Phoenix, Kathy Degner in Muscatine, Mary Kellenberger in Bettendorf, John Hrycko in Dowagiac, and Jane Walters in Rock Island...certainly, we cannot forget Mike Huang, at *Vine Line*, and Drew Litton in Denver.

A big thank you to Janell Hughes for her wonderful photography and to Jackie Paulus, Tom Langmyer, Jenny Stephen, and Ed Hansen at WGN Radio and the Tribune Company.

A tip of the hat to all those interviewed who missed the final cut—we just flat ran out of time and space. Over 20 stories were cut indiscriminately due to space limitations. It was close, and we're going to try to capture those stories in the next volume of *For Cub Fans Only*, Volume 3.

But the biggest thanks has to go out to the entire Santo family, especially Jeff for all his help. They were absolutely terrific... and fun.

FOREWORD

NAMESAKES ARE PEOPLE TWO

RON SANTO, JR.

Being Ron Santo, Jr. was a really good thing. I'm proud to be a 'junior.' Growing up was a little tough. There was pressure on me, obviously, having the same name and, certainly, playing baseball. There was always that. But, Dad never put any pressure on me when it came to baseball—ever. It was more me trying to live up to the name. When you're a young kid, there's the peer pressure. You can hear people saying "who is that?" and that type of thing. I could always tell, too, there were people trying extra hard to get me out because I was Ron Santo's kid.

There are always going to be people who try to compare you to your dad. Even when I play twelve-inch softball now, in my late forties, people who know who I am expect me to perform. Fortunately, I'm still athletic and can still do pretty good. There were times Dad said he regretted naming me Ron Santo, Jr. I can imagine how Pete Rose, Jr. was or anybody with the same exact name. Right away people are going ask "Is that any relation?" I always told Dad that there were many more good times that outweighed all that by far.

I realized early that Dad was different than other dads because every day of the summer my brother, Jeff, and I would go to Wrigley Field with him. Not many kids are going to Wrigley Field at nine in the morning and playing catch and fooling around with Ernie Banks and Billy Williams. Right then, you pretty much know that's not what the average kid gets to experience. This started when I was seven years old up until I was about fourteen, when he retired. We'd walk with my dad into the locker room and it was pretty much until the game was over, before he saw us again. People like Billy and Ernie were grabbing us and wrestling around with us. We used to help Yosh Kawano, the clubhouse manager, clean spikes, do laundry, all those kinds of things.

During the games we would explore Wrigley Field. There was a tunnel that went from the first base dugout to the third base dugout. It was dark and scary. One time we popped out and saw Willie McCovey smoking a cigarette and he looked at us like "where the .... did you kids come from?" When we told him who we were, he was nice and started joking around with us. We'd grab bats and play around with them. Heck, if I had known what the memorabilia market was going to be like thirty years later—wow. We had access to Mays, Aaron, McCovey, Clemente—all kinds of game stuff. We never did anything with it. One big memory I have is watching the game from the corner of the left field line where the old locker room was. How many kids can ever say that? We were, literally, two feet away from the foul line—just watching the games.

Going onto Wrigley Field and playing catch early in the morning with just my brother is a great memory. Wrigley Field used to have a net behind home plate that went all the way up to where the old press box was. That's where the foul balls would go up and roll back down behind home plate. Jeff and I used to play a game where one of us would have our back turned against the screen as the other threw the ball up toward the press box and yelled, 'turn.' You'd turn and search for where the ball was rolling back down the net—sometimes you'd make this spectacular diving catch, other times the ball would fly ten feet over your head—or hit the lip of the screen and drop down right in front of you. It was a great agility drill that could make you look really bad if you didn't locate the ball right away.

We never really tried to get autographs except for one that Jeff and I got from Hank Aaron on a baseball. We never were really into that. If I'd had a crystal ball, it would be different. We knew how it was on the other end so we didn't want to be bothersome and do that. We didn't hound anybody for autographs.

Ernie was so much fun. He was just that type of person. But, they all were great—Glenn Beckert, Don Kessinger, Billy Williams. That was one thing about that team. They were such great people. My dad and these guys were all actual friends outside the locker room, too. Jose Cardenal was a person who I really had fun with. He used to have that really big Afro and his hat just sat on top of it. He'd walk into the entrance of the locker room where it was all cement and start tap dancing for us. Sparks would fly off his metal cleats—it was pretty entertaining. Carmen Fanzone used to always do that beard thing on our stomach. He'd have a scruffy beard and he'd pin us down and rub our stomach and it would give us a red rash. We played catch with all these guys.

What I enjoyed the most was batting practice, trying to catch the fly balls out in left field. As a ten- or eleven-year-old, trying to judge a professional pop up out in left field was definitely a challenge. We did pretty well. We got better as we got used to it. When you're younger, those balls seem ten times higher than they do now. It took a lot of practice, especially when the Bleacher Bums were out in left field watching us. They'd always clap if we made a good catch. Dad told us, specifically, to stay in the outfield, which we did.

In '69, the Bleacher Bums were the guys with the yellow helmets. Everybody had their scorecards tied to strings like a fishing line. They'd hang 'em down to where the players who were running sprints on the warning track could sign and then they'd pull them back up. In that season, for some reason, a lot of people threw money, change—out onto the warning track. My brother and I would get plastic cups and collect cups full of quarters and dimes and nickels. I can't put my finger on why they did that but it was such a crazy season. There was also a guy with a megaphone at nearly every game leading the Bleacher

Bums' chants. After those games, on the ride home, fans would be everywhere. Dad would sign autographs at every stop sign on our route through those Chicago neighborhood streets, all the way to the Kennedy.

Watching from the left field locker room area, we had a unique view of the bleachers and the field. We'd always see Billy Williams, too, because he was in left field. Sometimes, he'd look over at us and give us a wink. I can still picture all of that like it happened today—the bleachers going crazy. We'd always try to be there for the ninth inning so that when the game was over, we could run out and watch the Cubs all walk into the locker room. That year, especially if they won, we'd always watch my dad click his heels. It was always entertaining to hear the crowd go crazy every time he'd go up in the air. That was a unique year.

I don't remember things turning bad that summer. By September of that year there were so many people just in tune, even our neighborhood. As a nine year old, though, I wasn't so swept up in when it started falling apart. I know my dad wasn't a happy camper but even other years—whatever year it was— if he didn't have a good game, it wasn't a particularly fun house to be in. Those were quiet drives home, too.

We would get out of school for spring training. That's a perfect example of when you know you're different than the average kid. We would be in Arizona the whole month of March. My mom would just get our work from our teachers for the whole month. The teachers would give them whatever work they were going to be doing back at the school and Mom would have a tutor help us in Scottsdale. We had a lot of good times. We always looked forward to spring training—not only getting out of school but going to warm weather and we loved Arizona. It was more fun in the old days at the game—spring training and Wrigley Field. When Dad was playing, we'd park at the gas station across the street from Wrigley and just walk to the door—that they still use—to go into Wrigley. Now they have a gated parking area. Then, though, he'd walk across Clark with us, signing autographs and talking. Literally, a lot of players parked across the street at this gas station—Vince Rizzo was the guy there and we knew him real well. He was a great guy. He owns it now but his dad was the owner back when my dad played. They became really good friends and they just watched the cars for the players. It's not a gas station now, it's a U-Haul rental place.

My dad would usually stay a couple of hours after the game. They'd sit around and talk—unlike today when the players shower and get out. After games, too, we'd be out there for a good hour or more while Dad was just sitting and talking and getting ready. Back in those days, they'd let kids earn a ticket for the next day by picking up old cups and folding the chairs up. You could hear the workers either stomping on the cups to make that popping noise and then throwing them in garbage bags, or they'd stack them up and have these really tall stacks.

We used to have fun with the Andy Frain ushers. That's when they wore the white gloves and hot uniforms in July. I can't imagine how they did that with the hats and the wool suits. We got along with a lot of those guys.

Dad was on the road a lot. It wasn't like Dad was the father who sat there and did homework with us, but the most important thing he did as a father was our knowing how much he loved us—that he would be there and would do anything we needed. He was by far the best at that.

The lake was like his personal driving range.

When we lived in Valley Lo in Glenview, we lived on a lake. Dad used to hit old golf balls into the lake. He would tee the balls up in our backyard and smack them into the lake. The lake was like his personal driving range.

I started doing that also, which was no big deal...except I didn't have the control he did. There were four neighboring houses down around the edge of the lake. If you sliced it bad, the ball would go into their yards. Dad told me to stop doing it unless he was out there to help me. ...but, one time I teed one up without him knowing and I sliced into this neighbor's yard. The neighbor came over and was not too happy. He threw out a couple of words my dad was not happy about. Obviously, my dad was much larger than this guy. My dad couldn't do anything to him...so, he took it out on me! That was not a good event.

Another time when my mom was out of town and Dad was watching us, he specifically told my brother and me to not get into trouble—to not cause any problems! I was 12-years-old, and that night, *I was brought home by the police.* A bunch of friends and I were ringing doorbells in an apartment complex and running away. Well, I happened to get caught because the front door closed. When the door closed, you had to be buzzed out again so I got caught. The local village police took me home. That was an event my brother remembers watching through the window—me being grabbed literally on the collar and raised up against the wall!

When Dad played, the memorabilia business wasn't big. People who did collect then did make a lot of money in later years because they were smart. I didn't really get into it until the early to mid-nineties. From then until now, my dad's popularity certainly gained a lot as he was announcing and became much more popular because of what he was going through with the leg amputations. People just identified with him. That certainly helped the memorabilia business on his end, too, as far as the demand for his autograph. It was certainly at its apex before he passed away. The most popular item the last couple of years before he died—which is kind of bizarre—was that black cat photo. The funny story behind that is that, for many years, people thought it was Glenn Beckert, which is crazy. I've always known it was Dad but about two or three years ago someone in the memorabilia business found out. I told them, "Yeah, that's my dad." All of a sudden, after that, it became the most popular photo that people wanted signed, especially the last two years of his life. It's so popular because of the '69 crumble and that photo was taken in Shea Stadium in the heat of the '69 pennant race—my dad's standing in the on deck circle and this BLACK CAT begins to circle him. Someone got a shot of that. My dad tells the story that the black cat, after circling around him, went to the edge of the dugout steps and stared right at Leo—then took off and disappeared somewhere under the stadium. That cat was the beginning of the end.

Dad went to a lot of memorabilia shows—he loved going and meeting fans. He was very, very appreciative when he went to those. He would shake everybody's hand; talk to people; never had problems taking pictures. He'd always tell whoever was the promoter of whatever store we were at that the most important thing to him was—that the public gets taken care of first before any private stuff for the store or the promoter in the back room. He always was very insistent that the public got taken care of. He had a very hard time if he had to get up after a couple of hours. He hated leaving anybody in line. A lot of times he would stay over the time limit where most players, these days, are up and gone.

If someone would come up to him in a restaurant and he could see them out of the corner of his eye and see that they were kind of hesitant to come over, he'd say, "Oh, c'mon. Don't be silly. You're not bothering me." He was not the type of person to turn anybody down. That's for sure. He'd go out of his way at times. Not many people do that. He just believed in treating people the same way that he wanted to be treated himself.

As long as I can remember, I do remember him taking insulin every morning in the kitchen, giving himself a shot in the stomach. I do remember—always—him taking those shots and having all the insulin needles in a drawer.

In late 2010, Dad told us that the cancer came back and the doctors said it was stage four and not curable. The doctors told him that if he didn't do chemo, he would have x amount of time. That pretty much gave us a punch in the stomach. We all thought that, hopefully, just like everything else, it can be taken care of. He might have to be in the hospital. But this was totally different. Of course, in the back of our minds, we were hoping that the chemo would slow it down and he'd go in remission just because of all the other things that he got through. But this was a little different because he said that it was past the point of no return. In the back of your mind, you don't want to think about what could happen—again—he always found a way to beat it.

He thought he could handle the chemo and so did all of us because he'd done so much before of getting through stuff that no one thought that he'd get through. We were keeping our fingers crossed that the chemo would work. The doctors were the only ones that were very worried about it. They truly knew what chemo is. We saw my sister go through chemo with breast cancer but she's also much younger and doesn't have all the ailments that Dad had. After the first week, we were concerned because we could see how tired he was. He just didn't seem himself so that was concerning. And, once the sugar levels start going crazy, like they were, that's what he was concerned about—being able to control the sugar levels which was hard for him. That's basically what started everything. Then it starts screwing around with the kidneys and then the heart.

The Cubs were just amazing how they handled the services. We can't thank them enough. I don't know another organization that would do that. The biggest thing, though, were the fans that stood in line on that cold day—Thursday—after the friends and family viewing. That really was emotional. We stayed a little longer to say thank you to some of them. That was when complete strangers were crying who didn't even know my dad personally. They stood out in that weather for two and a half hours. I'll always remember that as being unbelievable. I sit back and think who I would do that for? I don't really know. My dad would have been floored at the amount of attention he received. One thing that was so important to him was his relationship with the fans. When we did an autograph signing, he was always hoping that enough people would show up. He still had a little of that insecurity of not really realizing his popularity. That's crazy, now that I think of it. That's why he was so down to earth. It never went to his head like some people could have. If he would have seen all that happened at his services and the media attention that it got, I would hope that he would have finally realized how many people cared about him.

It really hasn't sunk in that he's gone. There are certain periods when I realize it like when I went out to the fantasy camp with Jeff. Then I realized it because he wasn't out in Arizona and he used to always come, even when he didn't play anymore and meet all the campers. Listening to the games and hearing Pat and Keith on the radio is hard because that's when my time was with him—from April to October.

As a father, Dad was the most generous father you could ask for. I don't think there are a lot of people who are as lucky as we were in that we truly knew how much our dad loves us. We knew we came first. I know there are many others who have parents like that, too, but, unfortunately, it is probably few and far between that you can say that about.

Even when we were forty, he still wanted to protect and take care of us. A lot of times issues would come up that we couldn't tell him because we didn't want to get him upset—we worried about his health. He would have felt like any problem we had would have to be on his shoulders.

We were concerned when my sister had cancer how he would handle it, but, surprisingly he was very strong. We were concerned that it would really bother him—would eat him up. That's how he was. We knew how much he loved us. He was the best father.

Chapter One

PAT HUGHES

Hear Me Now,
Listen to Me Later

PAT HUGHES

Pat Hughes was the WGN Radio side-kick of Ron Santo from 1996-2010.

My favorite Ron Santo story is the "Hairpiece on Fire" episode at **SHEA STADIUM***. It could have happened to anyone. It was 2003. The Cubs were in New York for a night game on a cold April evening. Right above our heads in the visiting radio booth at Shea was an old electric heater. Just a metal box, really, with a little tube in it that would glow a bright orange with warmth when you turned it on. We had it cranked up high on this particular night, and that baby was smoking hot. For the National Anthem, Ronnie and I respectfully stood up as the singer was performing. All of a sudden, I smell something burning. Then I hear this sizzling sound like bacon frying on the stove....ZZZZZZZZZ...Then I hear Santo say, "Shoot!", or a word that kind of sounded like "shoot." I looked over at Ron and I couldn't believe what I saw. When he stood up, he had gotten too close to that electric heater and his hairpiece had caught on fire! There was smoke billowing out the top of his head, along with a little blue flame. And he had this hilarious, confused look on his face. Well, I did what any good partner would have done. I poured a cup of water on top of his head and put out the flames. After a few seconds, the smoke stopped. Then I had to look away because I started to

*In an Old-Timers game at **SHEA STADIUM** in the 60s, Bobby Thomson homered into the left field bullpen off Ralph Branca.

laugh when I looked at his hairpiece. It had a big divot in the top! Ronnie always took pride in his appearance and he asked me, "How does it look?" I lied. "Not bad. Hardly noticeable, really. It doesn't look that bad to me, Ronnie." Hardly noticeable? It looked like Tiger Woods had taken a pitching wedge and whacked one right off the top of his noggin. What a great laugh we had—not only that night, but every time we visited Shea thereafter. The final irony to the story was something that always made Ronnie laugh. The name of the Mets starting pitcher that night was Al Leiter.

◇◇◇

The first time I ever saw Ron Santo in person I would have been about eleven or twelve years old. My brother John and I were big San Francisco Giants fans and we would often try to sneak into the player clubhouses at Candlestick Park. We'd always get run off by the security guards. They'd say, "Kids, you got no business here. Take a hike!" This one day in about 1967, the Chicago Cubs were in town and we had this bright idea. We figured let's jump on the field right after batting practice. We'll follow the players, hide behind their big bodies and we'll make it into the clubhouse. That's exactly what we did. One of the first people we saw was **ERNIE BANKS***. We recognized him instantly from collecting baseball cards and seeing him on television. He came up to both of us and could not have been nicer. He had a big smile on his face and said, "Hi boys. How're you doing?" He shook our hands and almost crushed them with his strong wrists.

We saw Billy Williams sitting quietly reading a newspaper. I knew the Cubs had played the Dodgers the day before because

*ERNIE BANKS became the first black manager—on an interim basis—in major league history after Cub manager Whitey Lockman was ejected in a May, 1973 game....Banks is an ordained minister and wed Cub pitcher Sean Marshall and his wife....Banks and O.J. Simpson are cousins. Their grandfathers were twin brothers.

I saw the game on television, and they'd faced Don Drysdale. So, we start pestering Billy with questions like, "What's it like to face **DON DRYSDALE***?" and, "Do you like hitting here at Candlestick?," and "What's your favorite park?" All the things a kid would ask a big league player. To this day, I still laugh and thank Billy Williams for not running us out of the clubhouse. He patiently answered our questions and then—after about two or three minutes—he said, "Who are you guys with?" I didn't know what he meant. My brother John was about three years older than me and he knew. John proudly said, "Our father's a professor at San Jose State." Billy didn't really look all that impressed by that. He said, "Oh, OK." We moved on and then I spotted Ron Santo across the clubhouse. Since I became his broadcast partner later, I would love to tell you that I met him, and talked with him and laughed with him, but I didn't. He was way across the clubhouse and he looked like a big tough ballplayer, which is exactly what he was. He wore these tight uniform pants and he just looked scary, to be honest. We knew who he was, though. We were just in awe of being in that clubhouse! We had just seen Ernie Banks, Billy Williams and Ron Santo! Every kid in America who was a big baseball fan in the 1960's knew those three guys. Then we saw Manager Leo Durocher come around a corner with a frown on his face and we got out of there real fast. We knew he would not be happy to see kids in there an hour and a half before game time. That's the only clubhouse we ever snuck into successfully. And we had tried many times before. And after. It is so sweetly ironic that the Cubs are the team that I ended up working for many, many years later.

---

*The late Buzzy Bavasi, when G.M. of the Dodgers, once offered his pitchers $25 if they would run a mile. **DON DRYSDALE** said he would do it right after Jesse Owens won twenty games....Drysdale said that his most important pitch was his second knockdown pitch. "That way the batter knew the first one wasn't an accident."

We were on cloud nine when we left there. We told people for years that we snuck in and met Billy Williams and Ernie Banks— like they were old friends of ours. But Ernie could not have been kinder and the same with Billy. I will cherish that memory for the rest of my life. In fact, it is almost surreal to be saying these words right now. I was just a shy, skinny kid growing up in San Jose, California who loved sports. I played baseball, basketball and football every day. Every single day. I wanted to be a big league shortstop, or play in the NBA or the NFL. But when I got be about 18 years old, I realized that I just didn't have the talent to be a professional athlete. That's when I started to dedicate myself to becoming a professional play-by-play man, and I worked at it night and day. And now I am in my 16th year as the "Voice of the Cubs." How did I ever get here? Amazing.

◇◇◇

I think that I always had a little bit of an affinity for the Cubs as a kid because the Cubs kind of reminded me of the Giants at the time. If you think about it, they both had excellent players, all kinds of future Hall of Famers, and they were extremely entertaining to watch and, yet, they never won the pennant. The Giants did win one pennant in 1962. The Giants had such talent. They should have won more than just the one. And the Cubs had Ronnie and Ernie and Billy and Fergie Jenkins and Glenn Beckert and Randy Hundley and Kenny Holtzman and Don Kessinger. The Giants had Mays and McCovey and **CEPEDA*** and the Alous and Jim Ray Hart and Marichal and Gaylord Perry. They had some tremendous teams. So, I think there was always a bit of a connection in my mind between the Giants and the Cubs.

◇◇◇

---

*Orlando **CEPEDA** used more bats than any player in history. He felt each bat had exactly one hit in it. When Cepeda hit safely, he would discard the bat. He had 2,364 hits in his career.

When Thom Brennaman announced in August of '95 that he was leaving the Cubs, I'd been in Milwaukee for twelve years and my broadcast partner Bob Uecker was not going anywhere. I decided that maybe I should try to move up a little bit. Make a little better salary; get a little better position and see what it was like to work in a big market. I thought that I could do it. I threw my hat in the ring, and sent some audition tapes to WGN radio. You never know when you try for a job in baseball broadcasting because the competition is so fierce. Everyone wants to broadcast in the Big Leagues!

I was both excited and nervous when I got the job, and very nervous for the press conference, but Ron Santo was there for me at the press conference. That was very nice of him. He didn't have to do it. Then, when my family moved to Chicago from Milwaukee, it was very generous of him to reach out as soon as we got to town. He invited me and my wife and two daughters out to dinner. He was so generous and that made me feel relaxed. Then the night before our first broadcast in Arizona, Ronnie called me where I was staying in Mesa and said, "Look, I know you're nervous. Tomorrow is your first game on WGN, but you don't have to worry about a thing. You're going to be great. You do the play-by-play, I'll do the color. We're going to have fun, this is going to be a great partnership. You just relax." He went out of his way to help me settle down and I actually was very calm for that first game. I will forever be grateful to Ron Santo for making me feel as welcome as he did.

The first game, top of the first, **MARINERS*** load the bases with nobody out against Frank Castillo. It's a long half inning. Ron Santo and I are working and discussing the strategy. We have a laugh or two, and then Castillo gets out of the inning. There

*During the Seattle **MARINERS**' first year in 1977, the distance to the fences was measured in fathoms. A fathom is 6 feet. For instance, whereas one park might have a sign that denotes 360 feet, the Kingdome sign would have the number 60...

was a pop-up to Mark Grace, as I recall, and the inning was over. Then I said, "At the end of a half inning, Mariners nothing and the Cubs coming up." Ron Santo stands up. He shakes my hand and the look on his face is that of a happy ten-year-old kid, as if to say "Not only was this fun for the first half inning, but OH, BOY, THIS IS GOING TO BE GREAT!" I'll never forget that look on his face. It probably was the same look that he had when a teammate would hit a key three-run home run as a Cubs ballplayer, or someone made a great defensive play. He just had that look of not only joy for that moment, but anticipated joy in the time that's still ahead. That was so much fun. I'm sure anybody who knew him well knows exactly the look that I'm talking about. I felt great, and that was the beginning of our 15-year run.

◇◇◇

When it came to Ronnie and the booth, he never was your normal broadcaster. I think that was part of his popularity. He was so unique! There has never really been anyone quite like him in the history of baseball broadcasting. For one thing, he never really understood what a "cough button" was supposed to do—what its role actually was. A cough button, for those that do not know, is used when the broadcaster needs to cough, or sneeze, or ask the engineer a question like, "Are we going to a commercial here, or are we staying live?" He hits the cough button so that what he says is dead and does not go out over the air. When you want to go back on the air, you let the cough button up and continue talking. Ronnie never really understood that. For one thing, he sometimes would mistakenly hit MY cough button, cutting me off for a few seconds, right in the middle of a play! He'd cough whenever he wanted to. He'd clear his throat. He'd blow his nose. He'd sneeze. The audience could hear him blasting his nose right into his napkin! All of this went right out over the air. Two or three times, he simply belched right out loud. Then he'd laugh and say, "Oh! Excuse me." I would try to cover for him by saying "apparently Ronnie has a story about Tim Belcher". He used his cough button only sparingly—or, by accident.

◇◇◇

People would write us letters, not just about baseball, they'd write Ronnie letters telling him that their own child was suffering. Ron would read these stacks of fan mail and he'd take them on the road with us. We'd be at the Great American Ballpark or Busch Stadium and it would be two hours before the game. I'd see Ronnie look at a letter and pick up the phone and make a call. He'd say, "Hi. This is Ron Santo. Is Mike Smith there?" Then I'd hear Ronnie chuckle and say, "No, this really is THE Ron Santo. Let me talk to your son." Then, he'd talk to Mike about his recent amputation or his problem with diabetes. He wouldn't just say, "Hang in there, kid." He would really talk to them. He'd say, "Listen to your doctors. There's a lot of medical advancement. You can live a good life and you can live a life of activity and achievement. Look at me. I've done it and I've been a diabetic since I was 18." Ronnie did this all the time. He'd reach out to total strangers and you know they felt better after Ronnie hung up the phone. The same would be with the kids that came to the booth with diabetes at Wrigley. My wife would bring her girlfriends who had daughters or sons with diabetes and Ronnie would say, "Check your blood sugar level. Make sure you exercise. Make sure you eat right. You can have a good life. Stay positive." It was really a wonderful part of his personality that he would always try to reach out and help someone who was suffering.

◇◇◇

Ronnie was on the phone one day with someone before a game. We realize that he's leaving a voicemail message. He's not talking directly to someone—you could just tell. He's looking at this letter that he's referring to, and he's saying, "I'd be happy to speak to your group." He said he'd be happy to talk about "Spam" cell research on such and such a date. I turn around to Andy Masur and Matt Boltz and say, "He's going to make a speech on stem cell research. He thinks it's 'Spam' cell. Now, THERE'S a speech I want to hear!" These guys fell on the floor. We're all howling with laughter. Just the thought of him speaking on this was enough to make you laugh, if you knew Ronnie. So he sees us, and hears us laughing, and he's right in the middle of leaving this voice-mail message, and he turns to us and says, "Oh, f--- you guys!" Then he realizes he's still leaving the voicemail and he says, "Oh, my goodness, Mary, I'm so sorry. But, I would be happy to make that speech and please call me at this number." Then he hung up. Then, we laughed even harder, of course. I don't know if he ever made that speech. I don't think he did. I would have paid big money to hear it.

◇◇◇

Thom Brennaman tells a story about him saying, "God d--- it!" right before he went on. Those were the first words he ever uttered on the air on Cubs radio. One night in Houston—around 2006—we're discussing a topic and I forget exactly what we're saying. I said, "Especially since the Cubs really need a win." And Ronnie said, "No s---!" I had two choices. I could have just let it sit there because I was kind of stunned, but what I actually did was just keep going. "And, the count is two and two and here's the next offering by **ROGER CLEMENS***, fouled away. Cubs trailing 2 to 1 here in the 5th," and just continued on with the broadcast. That way people could be thinking—"Did he say it or did I just imagine it?" It happens. These are live broadcasts. I'm knocking on wood that I've never done that. But, it could happen. It's one of the things that you dread but you hope there's that little tiny filter in your head that would prevent you from ever saying anything really bad on the air.

◇◇◇

*In July 2007 Yankee starting pitcher **ROGER CLEMENS** was older than five of the retired Yankees who played in that day's Old Timers game.

We would get these outrageous letters from listeners request-ing advice from Ron Santo. They would be about dating. They would be asking for advice on what to do about a sick dog. They would be about handling various problems. One lady writes a letter. She says, "Dear Pat and Ron, I'm an elderly woman. I notice the young ballplayers always seem to be grabbing themselves in the groin area during games. I want to share this with you. It's very personal, so I wish you would whisper this." Ronnie's reading this on the air and he says, "She wants me to whisper." "But, she says, I have a problem with 'femi-nine itching' and I really don't know what to do about it. Do you have any advice because you were a ballplayer and ball-players seem to have problems with that troublesome area, as well." He reads this right on the air and says the words "femi-nine itching!" As soon as he does, I say the words, "Ronnie, I'll see you tomorrow!" Then, he continues reading and she says, "Do you have any advice this area?" And, Ronnie says, "I think I do". Then, I say, "Ronnie, I'll see you next Sunday!" He goes on to describe that, "Ballplayers wear a jock strap. Inside of it is a cup. The cup moves around and that's why you see them grabbing this troublesome area." I say, "Ronnie, is that what's meant by 'starting a day from scratch'?" I'm trying to make light of it. As he's talking about it, I'm thinking "this is about as far out there as you ever want to be on a big league broadcast". Feminine itching. Only on Cubs Radio. Only Ron Santo.

◇◇◇

There is a frozen yogurt machine in the press box at the ball-park in Phoenix. There's a big sign on it. The sign says, "Do NOT turn this machine on until game time." Ron looks at the machine and figures, "I can't wait until game time. I have to broadcast." Click! He happily turns the machine on and fills

> We would get these outrageous letters from listeners requesting advice from Ron Santo.

up this big cup with frozen yogurt. Then to his shock and dismay, he discovers that he cannot turn the machine back OFF! Yogurt starts spilling out of the cup, on to the counter top. Ronnie starts shaking the machine trying to turn it off. He starts cursing. We all start laughing. He starts sweating. He's panicking. Now, yogurt is spilling on to the floor. There is a mountain of yogurt! It's an absolute mess. But instead of asking someone for help, Ron looks around and does what any mature 7th grader would have done. He simply RUNS AWAY! We could not believe it. Meanwhile, yogurt is still spilling out on to the floor. He's long gone. He figured, "Hey, that's someone else's problem. I gotta go to work. See ya later!" We all got a good belly laugh out of that one.

◇◇◇

My mom, Mary Margaret Hughes, of San Jose, California, is now 86 years old. She loved Ron Santo. She would listen to our broadcasts every single day on the Internet in the same house that I grew up in. She is one of the biggest Cub fans. Mom's nickname is "Granny." She loves that name. My two daughters call her that as do all of her grandchildren. She looks like a Granny. But, Ronnie would scold me for calling her Granny. He'd say, "That's not your granny, that's your mother. You don't call her Granny!" But she absolutely loved him. Whenever she was in the booth he couldn't have been nicer to her or any members of my family, for that matter. I thought my mom had a great observation of Ronnie toward the end of his life. She said, "You know, Ron is really teaching all of us older folks how to handle our physical problems. You don't complain. You just keep going. You stay positive. You try to have fun and you just keep on going until you can go no more." That's pretty insightful. Ronnie really was a huge inspiration for older people, the way he handled having no legs, having no bladder, being a heart patient and a cancer patient. He just kept going on and on with that great positive outlook with a lot of laughter. I think Granny really put it well when she said that.

◇◇◇

Another favorite tale is the Brant Brown story from late in the 1998 season. Brant Brown dropped a fly ball which allowed three unearned Milwaukee runs to score and dealt the Cubs a devastating loss. Ronnie's broadcast reaction is now famous in Chicago, and probably elsewhere, as well. As I'm making the call, I'm saying, "Brant Brown going back. Brant Brown drops the ball!" Right as I say "drops the ball", I hear Ronnie shouting in my headset, "OH,NO!" He said it, again, "Oh, no." It sounded just like he'd lost a member of his family. It was a horrendous loss. As soon as the game was over—at the moment the game was over—I look over at Ron—and his forehead is down on the table, like it's glued to the tabletop. He's not moving. I thought he'd expired right there! I jabbed him in the shoulder and said, "Ronnie, are you okay? Are you still with us?" He just said, "Yeah." He was really despondent over that loss. I finished the broadcast and did the postgame show. Ron goes downstairs to Manager Jim Riggleman's office. When I get there, Ronnie is sipping on a beer. It's probably his second or third by this time. He is still talking about the play. He's saying, "How could he drop the ball in that situation?" He's almost got tears in his voice as he's saying it. Then I see Jim Riggleman, the manager, walk over to Ron, put his arm around him and say, "Ronnie, it was a terrible loss, but hang in there. We're going to Houston. We can beat the Astros and still make the playoffs. We've got some more games. It's not over yet." I had to look away because I almost laughed out loud. I realized that I had just witnessed something that's never been seen in the history of American sports. I just saw a manager try to cheer up a broadcaster! Do you think Mike Ditka ever tried to cheer up Wayne Larrivee?! Do you think Whitey Herzog ever tried to cheer up Jack Buck? Do you think Tommy Lasorda ever tried to cheer up **VIN SCULLY***? I don't think

---

Once when Cub organist Gary Pressy was asked to name the finest singer ever during the seventh inning stretch at Wrigley, he unhesitatingly said "VIN SCULLY**."*

so. But, I will never forget that scene as long as I live. A manager trying to cheer up a broadcaster. Only with Ronnie.

◇◇◇

Ron had some problems with small booths. The booth in Milwaukee for visiting radio was really cramped and tiny. Ronnie was very claustrophobic. He could not stand to be in elevators. If an elevator would break down for a minute or two, he really was uncomfortable. He just wanted to get out of there. He also didn't like being in a car stuck in traffic. It was just one of his idiosyncrasies. It was really hard for him getting in and out of the old RFK Stadium before they built the new Nationals Park in D.C. You had to walk up a lot of ramps. It was really tough getting there. He would have a guy in a golf cart take him up as far as they could go but sometimes he'd have to climb up steps. He was so determined to be there every single day that, whatever the hardship, whatever the obstacle, he was going to be in that booth and he was going to broadcast the Cubs game. That's where he was the happiest in this world. And, by God, whatever it took, that's what he was going to do. It was unbelievable to see him climb up the steps to the airplane for our charter flights. He would grab the railing with his left hand. He would have his walking cane in his right hand. He had two prosthetic legs. He would just charge up the steps with this fierce look of absolute determination on his face. The same look he had to have when he was facing Koufax and Drysdale all those years ago. The man was driven to be in that booth and whatever it took—that's what he was going to do.

◇◇◇

One of the best weekends of his life—bar none—had to be the final weekend of September 2003. On Saturday, the Cubs swept a doubleheader from the Pirates at the same time Houston was losing to Milwaukee. It allowed the Cubs to clinch the Central Division Championship. It was the first time in Ron's career— and he was a Cub for 14 years as a player and that was his 14th year as a broadcaster. So, it was his 28th year with the organization—remember he was not broadcasting in either '84 or '89. He'd gotten to town in 1960. Finally in 2003, for the first time ever, he gets to be part of a division championship as either a player or a broadcaster. That was wonderful for him and he couldn't have been happier that the Cubs won the division. The next day was the day that his #10 was retired at Wrigley Field in a special ceremony. He gets up to speak and I had the honor of being the Master of Ceremonies that day. It was just surreal. The division champion Cubs; it's the last day of the regular season; the playoffs are going to start on Tuesday, but this Sunday Ronnie's going to have #10 retired. I said something like, "Ronnie and I love to tease each other but today is not the day to tease him. We'll do that later on. Today is the day we honor Ron Santo." He gets up to talk. First of all, he thanks the Cubs ballplayers for winning the division. That's the first thing on his mind! He says, "You guys have made my life so happy these last few months. Thank you. I love all you guys." Then he talked about what it meant to him to have his #10 retired. He said, "I want to go to the Hall of Fame someday, but to be honest with you, THIS is my **HALL OF FAME***, having #10 retired." If ballplayers in other cities might have said that, it would have had the ring of sour grapes. But with Ronnie, knowing how much he loved the Cubs, loved Wrigley and loved the fans, he really meant that. It really WAS his Hall of Fame. I don't know if going to the Hall of Fame, had it ever happened when he was alive, would have meant more to him than having #10 retired. I honestly believe that. Ronnie never used any notes when he spoke. He just got up and spoke right from the heart. That was just a beautiful speech that he made that day. Talking about "this is my Hall of Fame." It's something I'll never forget.

---

*The day after making his big league debut on June 26, 1960, the Cubs and Santo went to Cooperstown where the Indians and Cubs played in the annual **HALL OF FAME** game. The Cubs won 5 – 0 with Santo hitting a home run.

He and I were late getting to the booth that day because of the on-field ceremony, so Ronnie needed food because his blood sugar would drop and he had to eat something. We start the broadcast and he brings in a plate of scrambled eggs and a cup of coffee. That day, the State of Illinois proclaimed it "Ron Santo Day." He received a special proclamation paper—that special yellow parchment paper that you see under glass, in a frame on a wall. He gets this special paper and brings it up to the booth and puts it right next to his scorebook, right next to his scrambled eggs and coffee. He's broadcasting and eating, which is nothing new, he did that all the time. He gets excited and I look over and there's a big blob of scrambled eggs that plopped right onto the parchment paper. I thought, "Well, the proclamation means more to some people than it does to others." A little later he gets excited and spills coffee all over this proclamation. I thought, "Ouch. That's going to leave a real stain, forever." A few minutes later I look over at him and he's reaching for a napkin and can't find one. He picks up the proclamation as if he's going to scrape his face with it. I hit the cough button and say, "No, Ronnie, no! That's not a napkin, that's a proclamation! Don't do that." So he says, "Oh, OK." He puts it down and after I said that I'm thinking in the history of human language, how many times has that sentence ever been said? "That's not a napkin, that's a proclamation." I realize that it's probably never been said before or since. Later on, I remember asking him, "Ron, did that proclamation ever get up on the wall in your den or office?" He said, "Partner, I don't think it ever made it out of the booth that day." He threw it away! That was our Ronnie.

◇◇◇

He was one of the most horrendous backseat drivers ever. Jeff Santo was in San Diego for a road trip one time and he took us from the ballpark back to the hotel. It was a strange city to Jeff, and Ron was sitting in the front seat screaming at his son saying, "You're one of the worst drivers I've ever seen!" And

Jeff screamed right back at him, "You're one of the worst passengers I've ever seen!" He would direct you. He would tell you which way to go. He would tell you to speed up. He would tell you to slow down. He didn't like the way you approached stoplights. He didn't like the way you sped up after. It was amazing. He also didn't like other drivers. If someone would cut in front of us, Ronnie would think nothing of giving them an obscene gesture. Or, rolling down his window and actually shouting at other drivers. That was just him. Ronnie was a frightening driver himself. I always told him his driving reminded me of the name of the former Baltimore manager—Earl Weaver.

◇◇◇

The Texas Rangers have a guy named Elvis Andrus. Elvis struck out early in the game. I said, "Ronnie, I wonder if a pitcher, after he strikes out Elvis, isn't tempted to say—'You ain't nothin' but a hound dog!'" Ronnie looked at me and said, "What do you mean?" I said, "I believe that was one of Elvis Presley's songs." He said, "Oh, yeah, maybe it was."

Ron had a hard time with players' names. He ignored the Antonio part of Antonio Alfonseca. To Ronnie, the guy's name was "Al Fonseca". He gets him on an interview one day and says, "Al, I guess you've had shoulder surgery. You did have surgery, right?" Alfonseca says, "No." That's it. Just "no". Ronnie was not prepared for such a short response and he became flustered. Ron asks one more question and "Al" gives him another real short answer. Ronnie says, "Okay, that's it. We'll be back with more after this on the Cubs Radio Network." The whole interview goes about 25 seconds. It was supposed to go five minutes. It might have been the shortest pre-game interview in the history of the big leagues.

◇◇◇

At least once a week and sometimes two or three times a week, Ronnie would interview the manager—either Lou Piniella or Dusty Baker or Don Baylor—and he would come back up to the booth with a blank tape. He thought he'd interviewed them but forgot to press the "record" button properly, so he'd come up with absolutely nothing. It was comical how often this happened. Sometimes he would have to go back downstairs. Other times I would say, "Ronnie, don't worry about it. I'll cover for you. Let's just you and I discuss what Lou or Dusty or Don said and we'll be okay." It probably was partly because he had these gigantic fingers. I'm sure that's one reason why he was a great hitter. He had really strong hands and fingers. He just couldn't get that finger to hit only the "record" button. He would hit three or four buttons at once and would end up with nothing. As a result there would be nothing on the tape.

On one of our first trips in 1996, we were on a long charter flight back to Chicago. Ronnie has nothing to read, and nothing to listen to—no music or anything. So, he asks me, "Do you have any tapes I can listen to?"

I said, "Yeah, I've got *Bruce Springsteen's Greatest Hits*. It's a cassette. Here's the headset. Go ahead and enjoy, Ronnie." He says, "Thanks, partner." He goes up to his seat. He always sat in First Class. About 10 or 15 minutes later, he comes back and says, "I couldn't get your tape to work. There was nothing on it. I couldn't hear anything." Immediately, I thought, "Oh, no." I know what he's done. He's hit the record button, accidentally, and sure enough—I put it in play mode, rewound it, hit play and he has erased all of "Born to Run" and half of "Tenth Avenue Freeze-Out". Not only has he erased two of the songs on Springsteen's Greatest Hits, but he inadvertently recorded himself, and you can hear Ronnie's voice saying, "I can't hear anything." He's saying, "How about Hughes? He just gave me a blank tape to listen to! There's nothing on this dumb tape".

◇◇◇

Ron Santo welcomed a lot of us to WGN Radio in Chicago. There was me and Andy Masur and Matt Boltz and Cory Provus and Judd Sirott and countless ballplayers. He would go out of his way to make you feel comfortable. He also went out of his way to publicly say good things about you—which goes a long way with the audience. When an iconic figure and a hugely popular guy like Ron Santo says something good about you, it immediately gives you credibility with the audience. I will always be grateful to him for that because he went out of his way to say things like "Boy, you made a good point." Or, "You made a good call on that one." He'd say things like "As knowledgeable as you are, Pat, you know about the history of this team." Or, whatever it would be. I always will appreciate how kind he was in welcoming me and helping me to establishing credibility with the Cubs audience.

◇◇◇

Ronnie would talk about people being "different". The way he would say it would sound like "differnt". That's the way he would say it. He referred to a lot of people as "differnt" the first year or two I was around him. It might be another broadcaster. It would be a ballplayer, or another media member, or just somebody who came into our booth. "Differnt". It usually meant they were a little bit of an oddball; maybe a loner, or maybe they just wore different clothing. A funny thing about Ronnie was that he considered himself to be the standard of "normal". He thought he was the most normal man in America. So anybody that was not like him was "differnt". I thought it was funny when he would say it. Then he started finding out these things about me. One night we had dinner in Houston. After I'm done with a baked potato and I get all the potato out of it, I don't need the baked potato to be on my plate, so I put it to the side of the plate. One time I even put it into an ashtray. Boy, did he get all over my back for that. "You can't put a baked potato peel in an ashtray! You slob!" I said, "Okay, I apologize." Then he found out that I took duct tape with me on the road. I use it to keep the curtains shut tight because I don't like to be awakened by the early morning sunshine. So I use that gray, silvery tape to keep the curtains closed. Ron did not like that move at all and he scolded me. He said, "You don't put tape on the hotel curtains! These are nice hotels the Cubs stay in-you must be used to staying in cheap motels!" Then he found out that in real cold weather, I occasionally wear my socks to bed at night. He said, "Now, let me get this straight. You put potato peels in ashtrays, you tape the hotel curtains, and you wear socks to bed?" I said, "Yes, yes, and yes". He said, "Partner, I hate to say this, but you're real close to being differnt!" By saying "real close to", he let me know I was on shaky ground...yet, there was still time for me to change my ways and be "normal"—just like him, I suppose. I smile every time I think of that. "You're real close to being differnt!"

◇◇◇

He was my—unsolicited—Personal Behavior Advisor. One of the things about Ronnie that was endearing and hilarious, was the fact that he loved to tease you about your spending habits, or lack of spending, your table manners, your clothing—boy, did he get mileage on my sweaters! But, whatever it was, he would immediately bring it up and criticize you. And, he loved it when you would retaliate and criticize him right back. That was the kind of give and take he loved. I'm sure that was part of what the audience liked on our broadcasts every day—the fact that we would tease each other back and forth. Many times he would criticize an umpire for a bad call or criticize the appearance of an opposing player—maybe a long-haired ballplayer or a guy who had a weird-looking beard or facial hair that he didn't approve of or, maybe the guy was a little pudgy—whatever. If Ronnie would ever criticize an umpire or ballplayer, I would say, "Ronnie, I'm really sorry to hear you say that. I was reading an article the other day and the article was about this umpire and, somehow, the topic was favorite movies, and this umpire would say that his favorite movie was 'This Old Cub.'" Or, I'd say there was an article about this ballplayer and he talked about some of his favorite ballplayers and says he was a fan of the Chicago Cubs in the 1960's and, particularly, had a fondness for their third baseman, Ron Santo.

Ronnie was a good dresser and the irony was that he wore these really expensive shirts and pants and then he would spill his lunch all over them. I would always say, "It's not a big deal. It could have happened to anyone. And, fortunately, Ronnie lives right next to a dry cleaner, so it's no big deal." He was a mess, he really was.

◇◇◇

Ron Santo had an amusing habit of repeating what he just heard and passing it on to the next person. He did it over and over again. In Arizona, in 2001, this was right after Mark Grace left the Cubs as a free agent and joined the Arizona Diamondbacks. We're there for the first Cubs-Arizona game since Grace left. Before the game, Ronnie orders a pizza. The pizza delivery man comes in, and he says, "Mark Grace is a Cubbie. He should still be there in Chicago. He looks strange in a Diamondbacks uniform. Mark Grace should have finished his career with the Cubs. By the way, that'll be $15 dollars for the pizza." Santo pays. In the first inning, in Mark Grace's first at-bat. Ron Santo is on the air saying, "Mark Grace is a Cubbie. He should still be there in Chicago. He looks strange in a Diamondbacks uniform. Mark Grace should have finished his career with the Cubs." I look over at him in both amazement and amusement. He's quoting the pizza delivery man! I was thinking, "Thank goodness he didn't say, 'by the way, that'll be $15 dollars for the pizza.'"

Ronnie was about his funniest when he wasn't even trying to be. For example, he used to borrow my dental floss every single day. He didn't even know what it was called. He'd make the motion with his hands up near his mouth and he assumed I knew that he needed to borrow my dental floss. He owes me a couple of cases over the fifteen years. We're in Houston one night. He borrows my dental floss. I had cinnamon-flavored, it was red dental floss. It's during the commercial break and he uses the floss. Now, it's time to go back on the air. He quickly puts his headset on. He had those enormous fingers. Somehow the dental floss got stuck, and it draped over his ear and was hanging down the side of his face as he's broadcasting the game. I look at it and point it out to Matt and Andy and we're all laughing like fools. The first Cub gets on and gets to second and gets picked off. Ronnie still has this red dental floss hanging down. Ronnie is furious with the Cubs base runner for getting picked off. He looks over at me and says, "We've got to stop playing such stupid baseball! That is just foolish!" As he is saying this, he has this really angry look on his face, but he's got this red dental floss string hanging down from his ear and I had to look away. Otherwise, I would have just laughed in his face. He was sometimes at his funniest when he wasn't even trying to be.

At Houston during the 7th-inning stretch, Milo Hamilton, the Hall of Fame **ASTROS*** broadcaster likes to toss out bags of peanuts and Cracker Jack to the fans seated right below the radio booths. Ronnie and I had been watching this for years. Ron got the idea that instead of throwing out an entire bag of peanuts, why not just lean back, reach into a bag of peanuts, and throw individual peanuts out into the crowd? He did this, leaning back in his chair so that no one could see where the peanuts were coming from. This is during the commercial break, during the 7th inning stretch. He would lean back and just launch these things and then laugh like an 11-year-old. It was hilarious. I would stand up and give him the play-by-play. "That peanut right there hit an old man right in the forehead." Ron would laugh and throw another one. "That one seems to have landed in the hairnet of a woman and she's not real happy about it." He would just keep throwing these things. "That one

*On June 15, 1976, the Pirates were "rained in" at the Houston Astrodome. Ten inches of rain flooded the Astrodome parking lots and access roads. The teams made it to the park, but the umpires, fans, and stadium personnel did not.

landed in a little girl's cotton candy." He would laugh anytime I would say anything. He would just keep leaning back in his chair, throwing peanuts out into the crowd. It was something that you don't see every day in a big league broadcast booth.

◇◇◇

At one time, Ron was a scratch golfer.

My spending habits were often brought up by Ron on the air. Or, more accurately, my lack of spending. It originated to a golf game that Ronnie and I had with Steve Stone and one of Steve's buddies in Pittsburgh back around 1996. Ron was an excellent golfer. He had a beautiful, compact swing. He hit the ball right down the middle with power. He had a good touch around the greens and he was a good putter. At one time, Ron was a scratch golfer. He still expected to shoot right around par, as late as 1996. So, we're playing and, unbeknownst to me, we're playing in a money game. Santo and I are teamed up against Steve Stone and his partner. Ron has—for him—a very bad day. He shoots about an 84, to the point where he gives up on the back nine. He's not taking time on his shots and he's kicking the ball off the green when he misses putts. He's in that apathetic-golfer's-back-nine-mode that is very familiar if you've played much golf. Ron is just in a terrible mood. I, on the other hand, had one of the best rounds of my life. I shot something like 76. I'm rolling in birdie putts; I'm hitting every fairway. Everything is beautiful and I'm on cloud nine. I'm feeling as good as I've ever felt after a game of golf in my life—until, Ron Santo adds up the scores and the money figures. Ron is not happy as he adds up the scores and gambling results. He says, "We owe them $80 bucks." I was jolted back to reality! I said, "Eighty bucks? Each?!" As soon as I said, "each?", Ronnie exploded! "What do you mean, each?! You think I'm going to pay for you just because you had a good round and I played like s---? Yes, it's each! Now pay up—eighty bucks!" He was fuming.

From that moment on, to Ron Santo, my name might as well have been "Charlie Cheapo"! That was the start of him teasing me about my lack of spending. He didn't like the fact that I—after having a good round—maybe he thought that I figured that he was going to pay for me. That was not the case at all. It really was funny.

He would rip me, occasionally, for being a tightwad, thereafter. I would always come back by saying, "At least I pay for my cars." It was a running gag for about ten years, because Ronnie had a deal with Chevrolet, whereby not only was he paid a nice yearly salary to promote Chevys, he got a free car or two to drive every year. I used to joke and say that the last time he paid full price for a car, the big story in America was the Cuban Missile Crisis; or the big story in America was the Bay of Pigs. I would say, "Ronnie has been on full scholarship, room and board, ever since 1960." He got on me about being tightfisted, and I got on him about just waltzing through life on a free ride. It was a good gag and it was all in fun.

◇◇◇

Tyler Colvin is a promising young player for the Cubs. He had a good year in 2010, belting 20 homers as a rookie. The Sales Director at WGN Radio is a great guy by the name of Jeff Hill. He has a son named Tyler. Jeff and Tyler visited us in our booth in Cincinnati that season. Tyler's about ten years old and obviously, he's a baseball fan. I mention on the air, "Nice to have Jeff Hill with his son, Tyler, here. I say 'by the looks of Tyler, Ronnie, later on tonight if the Cubs need him, he could jump in there and pinch hit an extra base hit, no problem.'" I'm just having fun with the kid. The only things that Ronnie heard out of that statement were "Tyler" and "pinch hit". Ronnie proceeded to say, "Well, Tyler is not in the lineup tonight, but he is on the bench and you got three veterans out there right now. If Lou Piniella needs a pinch hitter later on, if that's what Tyler Colvin has to do, that's what he'll do." I knew where Ron was going with that as soon as he started it. He carried on for about a minute and a half. So, I turn around and wink at Jeff and Tyler Hill. We just wait for Ronnie to finish. He did, and we just moved on. To this day, every time I see Jeff Hill, I say, "Wasn't that a funny moment when he talked about your son and confused him with Tyler Colvin?" or "I will never forget your son's name!"

◇◇◇

I borrowed Ron's car in Milwaukee. I had to park it in the hotel parking garage which is on an incline. I thought to be safe, I should put the parking brake on so that the car wouldn't roll away. Ronnie goes out the next morning and, apparently, he'd never used a parking brake in his life. He did not know how to disengage the parking brake. He proceeded to drive from the hotel to the ballpark in Milwaukee at a top speed of 17 miles per hour! It took him about an hour and a half to take a trip that normally takes about ten minutes. When he got to the park, he was livid. He says, "Who put the parking brake on? Was that you? It took me forever to get here! What do you think you're doing?" We all exploded with laughter. Here's a guy who doesn't even know how to turn off his parking brake! He passed some Cub fans who were making their way to the park and he offered them a ride. They saw how slowly that he was driving and they said, "No thanks, Mr. Santo, we're in a hurry. We'll walk!" Here I am trying to do him a favor so his car won't roll away, and he gets mad at me. He drives all the way from the hotel to the ballpark with his parking brake fully engaged. I would think he might have ruined the car. But, then again, he got a free one each year, so who cares?

◇◇◇

Most ballparks play popular music on the **PUBLIC ADDRESS SYS-TEM*** between innings. One night a great oldie blared from the

---

*The **PUBLIC ADDRESS ANNOUNCER** for the Houston Colt '45s (later the Astros) in their 1962 inaugural season was Dan Rather...the P.A. announcer for the Brooklyn Dodgers in 1936 and 1937 was John Forsythe, later a TV and movie star.

speakers, and I said, "Ronnie, I never get tired of hearing 'Landslide' by Stevie Nicks." Ronnie looked confused. "Stevie Nicks? Who's he? I never heard of him." I said, "Ronnie, Stevie Nicks is a great admirer of the music of Billie Holiday." He said, "Oh. Billie Holiday. Now, HIM I've heard of!"

◇◇◇

He and I had a speaking appearance back around 2000 with the umpire Bruce Froemming. It's in the middle of winter, downtown Chicago. It was the day of a big snowstorm. I thought that the sponsors would cancel the event but they had tied up a lot of money, and logistics and rental of facilities and whatever, so they decided to go ahead with the event even though there was this big snowstorm. Ron and I take about two and a half hours through the storm to get from our houses to this downtown location. We get there and Bruce Froemming is waiting for us. When we start to make our speeches, I counted 56 people in the audience. 56! They're paying Santo, Froemming and me thousands of dollars in appearance fees and 56 people show up. Froemming had a great line when he got up. He said two things. He said, "I was going to say Ron Santo, gone but not forgotten. But looking at the size of this crowd, maybe he IS forgotten!" And, he says, "You know I've really never done a speech before where after the event is over, I can invite every single person there back to my room for a drink!" Santo was so embarrassed. Here he is, the marquee name on the event and nobody is there. Every time Froemming would work a game from then on, I didn't want to bring it up, but I felt that I had to.

That was another line I would use when I wanted to tease Santo. There would be something that I knew would be embarrassing to him. I would say, "Ronnie, I don't want to bring this up, but I have to, because I'm a journalist." It got to the point where I would say, "Ronnie, I don't want to bring this up..." and he would say, "I know. You have to. You're a journalist."

People have asked me if Ron and I rehearsed our discussions before going on the air. Not a chance. It's much more natural just to wing it and let it flow. It's more fun, too. In fact, now that I think of it, here is something amusing about Ron. He and I might eat lunch together before the game and discuss, say, an umpire's decision from last night's game. Then an hour later, we are on the air together. I would bring up the umpire's decision and he would say, "Yeah, we already discussed that earlier..." I felt like saying to him, "Yes, but we haven't discussed it yet ON THE AIR." But to him, the topic had already been covered-in the lunchroom! So I learned to make sure to NOT bring up anything beforehand that we could use on the air later. No, we did not rehearse.

◇◇◇

Ronnie would get confused with names. We were doing a television interview one time and he referred to me as "Bobby". I was "Tommy"—he used to work with Thom Brennaman, so maybe that was it. He called me Chris and Ed and maybe even Larry. I always felt that maybe I was the broadcaster to be named later. He would refer to people that he wasn't sure about their names, as "Big Boy". Like, "Hey, Big Boy. How you doin'?" He also thought it was really funny when someone would forget my name. Dick Vitale was in our booth one day before singing *Take Me Out to the Ballgame*, and he stopped by for a little visit with Ron and me. I introduced myself to Dick. I said, "Hi, Dick. I'm Pat..." and, as I started to say my last name, he cut me off. He said, "I know who you are. Everyone knows you! Don't worry about a thing." Then he goes on the air with Ronnie and me and he's doing his shtick—his "primetime player, baby, oh, yeah..." The inning ends and we say, "Thanks, Dick, for joining us. Have fun singing in a few minutes." Dick Vitale stops at the doorway before he leaves our booth and he says, "I just want you two to both know what a great thrill this has been for me to spend a half inning with Schultz and Santo!" With that he leaves. I think my jaw fell. Ronnie almost fell over with laughter.

Johnny Bench was on the air with us one time in Cincinnati. He says, "This is just great to be with you guys. Ron, I know how much you love the Cubs, and I hope you and your partner, Gary Hughes, have a nice time here in Cincinnati." Gary Hughes is a prominent baseball scout and a wonderful guy. But, he's not me. Ron thought that was just priceless that Johnny Bench called me Gary! Actually, I think it's pretty funny myself.

◇◇◇

We've had so many big names in that booth: Jimmy Buffett. Jerry Lewis. Russell Crowe. Kenny Rogers. Donald Trump. Shania Twain. Any number of ballplayers. Kirby Puckett was there just a few months before he passed. Ronnie would have one or two questions with these people, and then, if there was ever a lull in the conversation—since these people were going to sing *Take Me Out to the Ballgame* in honor of Harry Caray-, Ronnie would ask, "Did ya know Harry?". A lot of these people didn't even know who Harry was. Harry who? It became a joke. If they would say, "No, not really." Ron would go, "Ooooooh." That, to me, meant "end of interview".

◇◇◇

Ron was just a natural ballplayer. He was a great hitter and a great fielder. The game came easily to him. He just did everything by instinct. That's really how he kind of lived his life. As far as being detail-oriented and prepared, or a guy who planned out things, no. He flew by the seat of his pants. He had pure talent. He used to call his baseball playing "a gift". He realized how natural it was. I think that's why he was frustrated with so many current ballplayers, and even some of his teammates when he was a player. It was easy for him and he didn't understand why other people struggled so much with it. It's a very difficult game to play and there are millions of us who never even starred at the high school or college level that would have loved to. It's just a difficult thing to do. Baseball is a hard game to play really well.

◇◇◇

We would usually bail out on foul balls coming into the booth. Ronnie got hit right it the forehead one night in Houston. He just didn't see it coming until it was too late. I tried to lunge over but I couldn't get there in time. He wouldn't try to catch too many foul balls—especially later in his life. He couldn't see the ball. Houston was just a bad luck place for him. And, also, in Houston, one night they turned the air conditioning way up high. Ron had just a golf shirt on. So, by the second inning, he's freezing. I remembered that they had air conditioning in the park, so I wore a long sleeved shirt and I was fine. But I always keep this old wrinkled windbreaker in my broadcast bag. I've kept it there for about twenty years—just in case, you get on a bus, or a plane or an air conditioned stadium where it's much colder than you thought it would be. You put it on. It looks awful but it does the job. It keeps you warm. Santo, in the second inning, had goose bumps on his arms because he's so cold. I said, "Ronnie, I've got this little jacket here in my bag. You are welcome to borrow it." He says, "No! I wouldn't wear that thing if you paid me!" By the fourth inning, he's practically turning blue. And quietly he says, "Partner, can I borrow that jacket?" He puts on this rag and it's more wrinkles than it is jacket. It's hideous looking. If you could have seen the ashamed look on his face wearing my jacket in Houston! I wish I had a picture of it. He survived the game and, boy, was he embarrassed. You talk about someone doing something begrudgingly. He wanted no part of that jacket. He didn't care how few people saw him.

I had a back-up sweater in the booth at Wrigley just in case you woke up in the suburbs and it was 75 degrees and you got down near the lakefront at Wrigley and by the 8th inning of the game, it's 55. So, thinking it's going to be 75, you've got a short sleeved shirt on. Then in the late afternoon, it would turn cold all of a sudden. That's when I would put that sweater on. It was not a quality garment. It was very scratchy. It was like the last sweater on the bench, so to speak. That's why I took it to Wrigley as an emergency. It was awful looking. Every time

I would put it on, Santo would immediately criticize me for being cheap—"How can you wear that thing? Don't you have any pride?" One winter, someone broke into that little cabinet in our booth where I kept the sweater and they stole a bunch of items. They stole a headset. They stole a broadcast microphone and maybe some batteries. They let one thing stay in the booth—that sweater! Ronnie thought that was great. We got a lot of mileage out of that sweater over the years. Finally, Ronnie just grabbed it one day and took it with him. For whatever reason, he told me he threw it away at a car wash. Why at a car wash? He never explained.

◇◇◇

Ronnie used to brag about how handsome he was in his younger days. He really was a good looking guy, if you look at those pictures. He would brag about dating in his younger, single days. He'd say, "I dated nothing but tens!" I said, "That must be why you took that number to wear as a Cub because you considered yourself the male equivalent of Bo Derek." We got good mileage out of that. One day, his high school buddies from Seattle were in our booth. I said, "Ronnie here tells me that he dated nothing but tens. Is that true, you guys?" They all started laughing. They said, "I don't know about tens...but, at one time, he was dating five twos!" I said, "Ronnie, is that true? It does add up to ten, in a way." He said, "Oh, no, no. I dated nothing but tens." I said, "Are you sure it wasn't three threes and a one?" He said, "I never dated a one. Never!" The next time, his buddies from Seattle brought a picture in of one of Ronnie's dates from his glory days. Ronnie had been talking about what a pretty gal she was. It was a picture from when Ron was about 16 or 17 in high school in Seattle. This girl was NOT a ten. She was no more than a good, sturdy, three. I showed him the picture and said, "Ronnie, would this be one of the tens that you've been referring to all these years?" Oh boy, was he embarrassed. He says, "Well that wasn't really a date. That was just more of a friend. That wasn't a date." Sure, it wasn't. We had a lot of fun over that one. "Dated nothing but tens, boy."

◇◇◇

We're in a pennant race and playing the Dodgers in L.A., and one of the Cub players gets picked off first base. It's about the fourth time in a month this ballplayer got picked off. Ronnie is furious and he simply bellows out, "What is WRONG with that man?" I couldn't talk for a few seconds because I really wanted to just laugh out loud. I mean, that is funny! Here is a club's radio color commentator asking—loudly—about one of his own guys, "What is WRONG with that man?" I laugh every time I think about it.

◇◇◇

Late in the 1996 season, we get off the charter at O'Hare. We had wrapped up a 1-8 road trip. We were in a horrible mood. Everyone was down. We had been eliminated from the division race by the Cardinals. Somehow, as Ronnie is climbing down the steps of the airplane, his foot gets stuck in the shoulder strap of Ferguson Jenkins' garment bag—his carry-on bag. I don't know how it happened. They get to the ground, Ronnie's leg is up in the air, stuck in this shoulder strap. He's hopping around on one foot, cursing. Everyone is laughing and somehow he doesn't fall over. It was an amazing piece of dexterity and coordination. It was hysterical. I thought, "What a great athlete this guy is." It was amazing to see him hopping along for about ten steps with his foot stuck in this shoulder strap.

I was always happy when he would say, "You know, partner, you bring out the best in me." I'm sure that I could say the same thing about him. He absolutely brought out the best in me, too.

Sometimes Ronnie would be very quiet which was, simply, not like him. I knew he was experiencing a low blood sugar episode. He constantly would test himself by pricking his finger and drawing blood and testing his levels. He did that two or three times a day, every day. Sometimes, though, he would sag. We would be into the game and he wouldn't say anything, and I could tell that he was struggling. There was one night at

Wrigley about three years ago, in particular. He had this glassy-eyed look and I thought he was going to pass out. It was really frightening. Finally, we had to get a candy bar and a soda and I gave him one of my little granola bars that I carry for an emergency and we got that in his system and he was OK. He really suffered with that insidious diabetes. I knew many days when he got there that he was not feeling good. He was having a bad day or he had a bad night of sleeping. The traveling, alone, beats the heck out of you even if you're healthy and strong. I learned, because he had so many physical problems, not to complain about anything for myself. We all have problems. But, when I would look at him, all of a sudden, my own problems became almost nothing. They seemed to just pale into insignificance compared to his issues. No matter how much you are struggling, there's always going to be someone struggling more than you are.

◇◇◇

Around 1997, we have a night off in New York. We go to this nice Italian restaurant. It was one of those places that has a little bocce ball court right next to where people are eating. Guys are nicely dressed with their dates. After dinner and we'd all had a beverage or two, it's Ronnie, me, Jim Riggleman is there, Tony Muser, one of the Cubs coaches, and we're all playing bocce ball. We're just having fun, except Ronnie. Ronnie is treating it like it's the 7th game of the World Series. There's a big argument after every play and he's shouting. We're, literally, five feet away from these people that are having a nice, quiet, maybe even, romantic, dinner out. Ronnie is shouting, "Oh, bulls---!" And, "Son of a b----!" He's screaming these things out and these patrons are within arm's length of us. We're all laughing because we're realizing how embarrassing it is. That was Ron. He didn't seem to care that people were there. He simply cared about winning that game of bocce ball. We did not get invited back to that restaurant, by the way. It was pretty funny, though.

◇◇◇

People would ask if Ron would ever be in a bad mood. I'd say, "Of course, he would." But, it was almost always because the Cubs were losing. That's what made him grouchy. It was not that he was having problems with diabetes or his legs or low blood sugar—although, that had to be horrendous for him to deal with. The main time he was upset, grouchy, and in a bad mood was simply when the Cubs were not playing good baseball. That is a fact.

◇◇◇

One thing Ronnie would do in his later years which was almost too funny for words, and gave us all a big laugh in the booth—including Ronnie—was he'd take his headset off between innings. We would come back from the commercial break and I would put my headset on and start broadcasting. Ron would start broadcasting without his headset on. No headset equals no microphone! He would just be sitting there and talking as if he was analyzing the game. He'd be saying, "Well, this guy's got a real good slider. He's going to have to start throwing more of those if he hopes to win the game." You could faintly hear him through my headset. I would say, "Ronnie, that's a great point. I would love for our listeners to be able to hear. Would you please put your headset on with the microphone?" He'd laugh, "Oh, yeah!" Sometimes he would say it and you couldn't really hear it. I'd say, "Ron, you might want to put your headset on." Then, I'd say, "It's really a shame. Ron just made one of the more brilliantly, insightful comments in the history of big league broadcasting and nobody heard it because he didn't have his headset on." He did that at least twice a year that last three or four years. Just to look at him doing it was so funny you couldn't believe it.

◇◇◇

One of the most difficult assignments of my entire life was delivering Ron Santo's eulogy. Certainly I was honored to be asked by his family to do it, but I agonized over it. I had one week to prepare. I prepared for it every single night for an entire week. I would rehearse certain things in front of my wife Trish. And, she'd say, "Honey, I know it's going to be good." I'd say, "You know what, though? Ronnie and I had such a special relationship that I want this to be great. I want this to be something that the Santo family is proud of, and that Cub fans are happy with and might want to hear again in the future. I just want this to be great." Whether it WAS great or not, is not for me to say. I will say, however, that it is one of the very few things in my career as a public performer that turned out almost exactly the way I wanted it to. And, I know the Santo family was extremely happy with it. That was the only really important thing to me. I wanted Ron's family to feel that I captured him, and I sincerely hope that I did.

I was interviewed by dozens of people after Ron died. One question that came up more than once was, "Could you summarize him in one word?" No. He was too multi-faceted for that. As I said during the eulogy, "Many words and phrases come to mind when I think of Ronnie. Let's start with unique and unforgettable...courageous, inspirational...natural, genuine, generous and charitable...loyal, strong, and tough...optimistic...outrageous and hilarious...loud...nosy...forgetful...a fashion cop...a food cop...backseat driver...#1 Cubs fan ever...a partner, and a friend."

"Ron Santo and I enjoyed an unusual chemistry on the air, and we had a 15 year run together. We covered some pretty good Cubs teams, including four ballclubs that advanced to the postseason. But our broadcasts were always about more than just baseball. We laughed every day! He taught me a lot about the game, but more significantly, he taught me how to laugh at myself. And that is a very important lesson to learn."

Toward the end of the eulogy, I said something like, "Whatever memories you have of Ron Santo, I know it would have pleased him very much if you try to remember him with a big smile on your face." I think the last line was, "In these past few days, it's as clear to me as it has ever been, that for these last fifteen years with Ron Santo, I have been a part of something very special. Thank you."

◇◇◇

He would mispronounce names on the air. There was a guy named Carlos Baerga and Ronnie would refer to him as Carlos "Viagra". He said that on the air many times. I said, "Ronnie, why don't we just call him 'Old Carlos', from now on?" One time he tried to say the word retroactive, as in "...this player is on the disabled list retroactive to last Saturday." It came out "rectal-active". People thought he was doing this on purpose for a laugh. I promise you that he was not. One time in the middle of a wild play where two Cubs ended up on third base at the same time, in my headset, I hear him scream out, "J---- ------!" right in the middle of my play-by-play. You don't hear that every day.

Ron and I posed for countless photos with fans over the years. When he starting using the prosthetic legs, the photos became painful experiences at times-for me. We would be standing next to each other, and he would accidentally be standing on the top of my foot. Obviously, he couldn't feel his feet, but those prosthetic legs felt like a croquet stick digging into the top of my foot. I am trying to smile for the picture, but I almost have tears in my eyes from the pain. It was a combination smile/grimace! When the photographer finally snapped the photo, often I had to let out a little yelp of agony. Good times.

◇◇◇

There was also a fan who wrote an e-mail to us when we were down in Florida. We were talking about the Everglades and alligators and crocodiles and I said, "Matt Boltz, why don't you type up something on the Internet there and give us the difference between alligators and crocodiles." He prints it out and gives it to Ron to read on the air. Ronnie starts reading and he says, "Alligators have a real broad 'snot." I said, "Ronnie, do you think that might be a broad 'snout'?" He said, "Oh, yeah, maybe it is." We both just started laughing. Ronnie couldn't even talk for about three minutes. A broad snot.

◇◇◇

We would get letters, faxes, e-mails from people from real small towns. We would ask, "Where is that? Have you ever heard of this town?" For example, Chicken Creek, Illinois. I'd say, "Where is that, Ronnie?" He'd say, "I don't know." We'd have Matt Boltz print out some information on Chicken Creek and he'd hand it to me and I'd say, "Well, I'll be darned, Ronnie. This is going to surprise you. Chicken Creek is a town of three million people!" And, he would say, "Really?" Then, I'd say, "Oh, wait a minute. It's a town of thirty people. I misread the zeroes." But he actually would say, "Really?" He was so charmingly gullible.

Every year at Christmas, he would be very generous and send my family either a turkey or a ham. I got him on this one for five straight years. As soon as I got it, I would call him to thank him. I'd say, "Ronnie, thank you very much for the turkey. By the way, I've got a couple of neighbors who are really turkey lovers. Could I give you a couple of more addresses?" Then, he'd say, "Whatta you mean?" Then, he realized that I was joking and he'd laugh and laugh. Or he'd send a ham and I'd say, "Listen, Ronnie, I really appreciate this ham. Thank you very much. But, we're having a big party. We're having about twelve people coming. Could I possibly get about three more of those things?" Again, he'd say, "Whatta you mean?" He would not realize right away that I was joking.

I'm very happy to be a part of fifteen years of Cubs history with Ron Santo. I love baseball history and it makes me feel good knowing that many, many years from now, long after I'm gone and when my kids have their kids, some people will still remember "Pat and Ron". I hope they remember us fondly. It makes me feel happy to think I've been a part of the WGN Cubs baseball broadcast history.

I am sure I will never meet anyone ever again that even remotely reminds me of Ron Santo.

IF THE PHONE DOESN'T RING...
IT'S THE HALL OF FAME

KERRY WOOD

Kerry Wood was Ron Santo's favorite player. He shook the baseball world in 1998 as a 20-year-old rookie by striking out 20 Astros, tying the Major League record for a 9-inning game. Wood was the National League Rookie of the Year in 1998. In the 2003 playoffs, he earned two wins vs. Atlanta in the Divisional Series, including the Game 5 clincher. He currently works in the Cubs bullpen.

I wrote an article about him for **ESPN***—the Magazine. The editors came to me and asked if I was interested in doing it. I did research and compared his numbers to all the Hall of Fame third basemen, put his credentials up against all the third basemen that are in there and wrote an article what he'd been through and what he was as a player and how his numbers stacked up against these guys. It was my little argument, my little pull to get him into the Hall of Fame.

I would watch the Cubs when I came home from school. Obviously, by then, Ronnie was announcing. I didn't know much about Ron Santo until I got to Chicago and figured out, real

*There have been almost 400 self-serving *SportsCenter* commercials. The only athlete to turn down an **ESPN** ad was former Cub, Bill Buckner. ESPN wanted to shoot him alone in a utility closet covered in dust. An anchor would open the closet, push some mops aside, and there would be Buckner. The anchor would ask Buckner if he was okay, and Buckner would say, "No, I'm not good." The anchor would then turn out the light and walk away.

quick, what he meant to the organization. He was always one of the first guys in the clubhouse. I would have a conversation with him on a daily basis—every morning. Honestly, very rarely was it about baseball. It was always fun and we always had a good time together. I got a chance to see a side of him that very few people got a chance to see.

We had conversations every day and we talked about life, his grandkids, my kids. He was an old-school kind of player. When I came up, I was an old-school kind of player, even as a rookie. I kept my mouth shut; paid attention; watched what everybody else did. I watched how everybody went about their business and handled the media as best I could. I tried to very humbly handle the media in the spotlight that I was thrown into. He probably appreciated that being from the old school way that he came from. A lot of times nowadays, with the younger players—you don't see a whole lot of that. There was something about that that made him like me.

We all wanted to say that we knew what Ronnie was going through because we got to see it every day, but I don't think we had any idea. We saw a tenth of what he was going through. We never heard him talk about it or complain about it. For me personally, being in the Cubs organization, getting drafted by them, you have a special relationship with the organization that brings you into the big leagues. There's a loyalty there for me, anyway. I knew how much the Cubs meant to him as a player through all those broadcasts and how much it meant to him in 2003 when we had a great season and he couldn't make it to a lot of the postseason and he couldn't make it to Florida. I just remember saying that he's got to be there, somehow. Hanging his jersey in the dugout every game wasn't just my idea. Walking off the field after winning Game 5, someone handed me a phone and it was Ronnie on the other end of the line. I got to spend a good twelve minutes walking down the tunnel talking to Ron about what had just happened. I'll always be elated for that. I hadn't shook hands with anybody on the team, yet. I hadn't high-fived—no champagne. I got to hear his emotions and that was so special. He really was out of words. He was emotional. He was extremely excited. We all knew how he sounded when he got excited. Times that by three or four—he was almost speechless—just very emotional and that meant a lot to me.

We didn't talk a lot about it, but I think he mentioned the following year that it meant a lot to him that we talked, but we really didn't talk about it a whole lot after that. I appreciated it more than he did and more than he could imagine. It was special for me to talk to the Cubs legend right after the game and have him share his emotions with me. All the games that he's seen in a Cubs uniform—WOW!

> We all knew how he sounded when he got excited. Times that by three or four.

I've got the tape of the game where I struck out twenty batters. I've got the one of Ron and Pat doing the game. The emotion and excitement of that game was awesome and something I'll always hang on to. I want to my kids to hear it. I don't know if Ron did anything different in the game but it's fun listening to him.

At the funeral service at the church I came in to see the family. Obviously, the line was full of Cubs personnel and front office employees. I started to talking to many people I hadn't seen in a few years. I was a free agent at the time and was still hearing from a couple of different teams. I hadn't really thought about the Cubs—it really hadn't crossed my mind. My wife and I started chatting with people in line and catching up—talked to Jim Hendry and ex-players, a lot of the people that I've known for the past twelve years. I'm seeing a whole section of fans at the service. Obviously, Ronnie had a special relationship with the fans but I knew three-quarters of the fans that were sitting in there. I thought, "Lord, this is what being a Cub is all about." You've got all these ex-players, all the personnel and you've got a whole section of fans who grew up watching this guy and here they are at his service. You don't get that with anyone else. Where else are you going to get that with any other team? So, that to me, is just what being a Cub is all about. It's just different. I had a conversation with my wife on the way home about how special the Cubs and their fans are. Later on that night I had an event to go and ran into Jim Hendry again. We basically just said, "Let's get something done." Two days later we signed the contract. That's how it happened. Ronnie had a lot to do with it, obviously.

Cubs fans are special. There are 40,000 Cubs fans at a game on Tuesday at 1:20. They're sold out in the middle of the week. It just a different atmosphere in that stadium...in that ballpark... around the stadium. And, these fans travel. They go all over the country to watch their team. It's similar to the Yankees but there is a passion there from many, many, many generations. People hate to hang on but they hang on because they know what it's going to be like when we finally do win it. They follow us around the country and pull for us.

When I got drafted by the Cubs, I was 17. I graduated high school and the next thing I knew, I was in Fort Myers...and I'm a Cub. It happened that quick. This year will be my 17th season in pro ball and 15 with the Cubs. Sometimes it seems like it was yesterday. I guess the older you get the faster it goes.

When I think of Ron Santo, a smile immediately comes to my face. There was not a more positive man. Even when he was irate, he made me laugh. There's not a more positive human being on the planet that I've ever come across. And, he had more reason to be negative than anyone I've ever met. He had a special heart and was just a special human. Not only Cubs fans but baseball is going to miss him, the organization is going to miss him and I'm going to miss him. I was sitting at his service and I don't really want to laugh but I can't help it. That service could have gone on for three weeks with people telling stories. I loved him.

Ron and Vicki Santo with close friends Carol and Ray Scarpelli

Chapter Two

ALL IN THE FAMILY

LIVING WITH A LEGEND

VICKI SANTO

The former Vicki Tenace was married to Ron Santo for 28 interesting years. She has been a world-class equestrian, training in Scottsdale and Chicago.

We met at a stable in Northbrook, where we both kept our horses. Ron moved his horse in when I was in England visiting my sister, so my friend Dee Dee met him before I did and introduced us. Ron had heard that the horse I had was very fast and tried to arrange a race with Dee Dee. She didn't want to risk any injuries to my horse so she told him she was sure I would race him when I got back. After the introduction, he said that Dee Dee assured him I would be willing to race down the trails. We arranged a time for the race but Ron showed up with a new horse off the track claiming that his horse Mariah was lame. The trails we raced on were no more than 10 feet wide and very winding. We flew down the trail and luckily did not run into anyone coming the other way. At the end of the race that was a close one, Ron said "I am so impressed you can keep up with me." Little did he know I rode every day and had won the world championship pleasure division in 1969 in Louisville, Kentucky.

Ron and I were looking for an activity we could both enjoy. I knew that I didn't want to golf with him because he was a 6 handicap at the time and I didn't play. We chose **TENNIS*** because we were probably fairly matched on the court. The first day we went to play, as we were walking to the courts, he said to me, "Once we cross these white lines no one is my friend". Who says that to someone they hope to have a relationship with? I belonged to a tennis club, and Ron and I played in a doubles group. They were having a round-robin tournament and we decided to play in it. We were really the underdogs but Ron was so quick at the net, not much got by him. We ended up going much further in the tournament than we should have with our ability—in typical Santo fashion, Ron would jump the net if we won. I don't think that endeared us to the rest of the players. It was probably a carryover from the days of clicking his heels after a win at the ballpark.

Ron had already retired from baseball when we met and was in the residual oil business. We were really good friends for a long time before we married. I met his '69 teammates at Randy Hundley's first fantasy camp. His teammates were a very close group and really fun to be around. They teased each other with no mercy and still to this day are wonderful support for each other. Ron was such a nice person, so real, but he didn't realize how funny he was. After spending time with his teammates, and seeing the way they teased each other, I realized that it was a loving way of keeping each other grounded. They all left their egos at the door when they got together.

After we were married in '82, my daughter Kelly was having her twelfth birthday party at the Palladium in Glenview, then back to the house for a sleepover. Ron and I each had a car full of girls to drive. As we leave for home he tells me, "We will be home before you." As we get near the house, I was in the lead

*In what sport was Chris Evert the leading money winner in 1974? The answer: Horse racing. The owner, Carl Rosen, named his horses after **TENNIS** players. The horse named Chris Evert won $551,063 with five wins in eight starts.

so as we get to the yard, Ron cuts across the lawn to be in the driveway first. Lots of cheering from his car full of girls and lots of "YOU CHEATED" from my girls. I guess second place was never good enough for Ron.

It was horrible riding in the car with Ron driving. He never knew where he was going. He was supposed to go to a pumpkin festival for WGN one autumn. He left the house and called me a half hour later screaming, "I don't know where I am." I said, "You are calling me to ask where you are? I am home in the family room and you're calling me to ask where you are? You are kidding, right?" He said "I don't know where I am and I was supposed to be there half hour ago." I asked about cross streets and if he knew the address. I then suggested he do what men hate to do, stop at a gas station and get directions. He eventually got home but the blood pressure was sky high for the day.

Because of diabetic changes in Ron's eyes, he had lots of laser treatments. Over 5000 burns in the left eye and the same in the right eye. As a result, his night vision was not very good and it took a long time for his eyes to acclimate from light to dark when he went into a movie theater. We went to a movie one off day and the theater was really crowded. We tried to wait at the back of the aisle for his eyes to adjust, but this one time the movie was ready to start so we walked down to a row of seats. I told him there were two seats all the way in and to follow me. The hearing must have been going, too, because he went in two seats and sat down. Unfortunately, there was a very old man already sitting in that seat. He very kindly said "Two more down, pal." How embarrassing was that? We have told that story for many many years.

As Ron's health issues became more severe, he accepted his journey with great dignity and courage. We would go out to dinner weekly with our dear friends who would listen to every medical report and were so very supportive of all that Ron had to deal with. One dinner Ron was being teased as usual, and he turns to me and said "That does it, we're done, we are getting a divorce." I started laughing and said "We could do that, but I will have to send an owner's manual with you, how to work the prosthetics, pacemaker, hair piece etc." His next comment can't be put into print, but we all had a good laugh.

He had always loved dogs and our border collie Duke had died right after Ron lost the right leg. I got an Australian Shepherd from a breeder in Canada. His name was Joker and he was two years old when we got him. Ron would spend quite a bit of time on the air complaining that JOKER HATED HIM. He was such a sensitive dog that if you sneezed or coughed, he would leave the room. Ron was such a large presence with a booming voice that Joker just couldn't handle it. After complaining one day on the air during a slow game, a dog psychiatrist called in and told Ron that dogs like Joker are very sensitive and they pick up on your energy. He told Ron that after a loss at the ballpark he should go home and have a glass of wine in the closet. Just do that and don't come out or talk to the dog until after you have settled down.

As time went on, our sensitive Joker saved Ron's life many times. Ron tested his sugars religiously but there would be times that his sugars would drop so rapidly that he couldn't get to the orange juice. Joker would come and get me, wherever I was. Once I was in the backyard, another time in the basement. He came and puffed and panted until I followed him to find Ron in real trouble. I noticed this more and more. If anything went wrong—anything that was not right—the dog would come and get me. I took Joker to get his public access certificate so he could go anywhere with us...even in the plane when we went back and forth to Arizona.

In October 2010 the doctors suspected that the bladder cancer had come back. Ron went for an ultrasound and before we got the results I noticed that Joker would sit with Ron in the living room. That was very unusual behavior for him unless Ron had food in his hand. We were discussing the possibility of chemo if it was cancer and Joker went over, sat next to Ron, and put his paw on Ron's knee. Ron just looked at me and said, "He knows." He was right; Ron had stage 4 bladder cancer.

Ron was willing to go through chemo but he did not think he would be able to make it. On December 3rd, his kidneys failed as a result of the chemo.

During the funeral I left Joker with a friend who had lots of dogs. When we came home from Chicago, Joker was limping, but I thought he had just played too hard with all the other dogs. He wasn't better after Christmas and exactly five weeks after Ron died, Joker's kidneys shut down from cancer. He had never had a sick day in the six and a half years that he was with us. He had regular vet checkups and blood work done. I had to put Joker down that day and I knew in my heart that Joker was here with us, to help me, help Ron through his illness and all the frustrations that came with it. The fact that he died of the same kidney failure, told me that his job was done and he went with Ron to the afterlife.

Life was never, ever, dull around Ron. He was an amazing man who showed courage, determination, and love of life. Hopefully all who knew him feel that they are better people for having known him. I know I feel that way; my life will never be the same, but what I have learned through my journey with Ron has made me a stronger person.

THE SON ALSO RISES

JEFF SANTO

Jeff Santo was born in Oak Park, and resides in Phoenix. He is a filmmaker, President and owner of Santo Films (www. santofilms.com). He served as the director/producer/writer for his 2004 documentary on his dad, This Old Cub, *which won numerous awards and is the top selling DVD in Cubs history.*

Growing up with my dad, the only thing I knew was going to Wrigley Field with him in the summer time and leaving school for a month and going for spring training. Ronnie and I were spoiled in that way, and didn't know any differently. That was our norm. We got tutored twice a week in Arizona when we went to spring training. We had two days of class and the rest of the time we were going to the ballpark with our father.

I look back at those days and it's like beautiful, nostalgic scenes out of a film. That was an era that's gone now. The whole Cub team used to stay at the Ramada Inn in Old Town Scottsdale for spring training. That was unique in itself. You'd go to the coffee shop and see Ernie, Beck, Kessinger, my dad having breakfast before going to the ballpark. A lot of them would walk to the ballpark. It was that close. It was unique. If you came to the pool at the Ramada Inn back in 1969, all the guys would be poolside with their families. You don't get that anymore. We were like one big family, and that was beautiful.

We were all so close that you didn't think of them as ballplayers, so I didn't have a favorite Cub. Usually my favorite player was on another team. At one time, Roberto Clemente was my favorite player. Dad laughed about that because, "Who didn't like Roberto Clemente?" When you are around the players and get to know them so well, it wasn't like, "Oh, I idolize Ernie Banks." I see *him every day.*

> To me and my brother, Wrigley Field was our playground.

To me and my brother, Wrigley Field was our playground. We would roam that ballpark. We knew every inch of that ballpark. We'd hang out with the firemen across the street during a game, slide down the fire pole. Everyone around the park brought us in. Leo Durocher would be like, "Hey the game's going to start in about half an hour. Get the ---- out of here." We're gone.

Back when Dad played, the clubhouse was in the left field corner, and it wasn't underground. Wrigley was unique for that. People didn't realize that. Underneath the dugout was a pit. There was this little urinal. Then you go back a little farther and you either go into the concession area or you could make a left, like my brother and I would often do. There was a dirt pathway that had a lot of old equipment and was right off the umpires' room. I felt like we were in the "Goonies" searching for the lost treasure.

You would go into this little hole and it would take you to the other dugout. When we discovered that, we went crazy. You would go all the way through this tunnel of rats and make this journey to the other dugout. Milt Pappas' kid would hang out with us. He and Ronnie were the same age, and I was the little young guy who hung out with them. Like, if the Pirates were in town, they would lean their bats against the wall of the dugout. These guys would take their bats and then would sell them. I'd be crying, "You can't do that. Dad will kill us." We never got caught. They would also take cigarettes. At that time, a lot of the players would go under the dugout back where the cameras could not see them, and they would smoke. They would keep their cigarettes on a little ledge there, and we would take them. One time a player tried to chase after us, he had no chance, that tunnel was made for kids.

Later on in life, we told our dad what we did, and he laughed about it. We grew up in all that stuff. We were finding ways to entertain ourselves other than the Cub baseball game.

You could actually go outside Leo's office and be underneath the concession area. Joe Pepitone used to drive his Harley through Leo's office. He would drive it through his office and park it in the locker room. It was crazy. Back then, it was a different world.

That was when Dad wound up clicking his heels because after the game they would have to walk down to that left field door. One game Jim Hickman had hit a home run, then Dad ran down and clicked his heels out of excitement. They got it on the WGN camera and showed it that night. They kept playing it over and over so when Dad came to the ballpark the next day, Leo said, "We're going to make that our victory kick. Can you do that after every game we win, Ron?" So it got to where everyone would wait around after the game for him to click his heels. Naturally they would walk down to that left field corner after a game. Sometimes my dad would sprint down after they would win—you would see him sprint down to that door. My brother and I would watch the games out of that door.

For *This Old Cub,* I wanted footage of my dad clicking his heels and at first didn't get that much. When I was in town just before his funeral service, my wife and I watched WGN do a tribute to him. They showed him clicking his heels. Then they showed him running and actually disappearing into the locker room through that door. You could see me and my brother as kids standing there. I said, "Oh my God, that's me and Ronnie." I had never seen that footage before. I saw Marc Brady, the producer for the WGN Cub games and said, "You've got to get me that footage for the new edition." Ronnie and I, as little kids, are right there as Dad walks in after he clicks his heels.

The Cubs players never parked in a section that was blocked off like it is today. They would park at a gas station across the street, Vince's Gas Station. You can see it in old footage that I have in *This Old Cub* where Dad and I are walking. We'd drive in and park at the gas station, walk across the street, with Dad holding my hand, and go in through the administration entrance and walk to the clubhouse all the way to the left field corner where the clubhouse was. I remember those walks so well. The reason the players parked there, the station would service their cars and have them ready for them when they got out. There wasn't a real players' lot back then.

When Dad would walk to his car, he would sign autographs, and then we'd take back streets before we got on the Kennedy to get to Glenview, a north Chicago suburb. On these back streets, at every stop sign, there would be kids waiting for him wanting his autograph. He took the same route home every time so the kids all knew that. On one of these back streets, there was an old tavern where he would stop, leave Ronnie and me in the car and go in and get two beers for the ride home.

We went to most games at home in the summer unless we had a baseball game ourselves. My dad had a thing with us. If, on the way home, we were able to count 50 Volkswagen bugs, we would get to miss school and go to the game the next day. We'd be yelling out the numbers and the colors and keeping count. That was our way of getting a free "hall pass" to the game the next day if we counted 50 bugs on the way home. He would always give it to us even if we might be 3-4 shy. Only when they won did he ever give that to us 'cause when the Cubs lost, it was not an easy ride home. When we lost, we'd be like, "Can someone else give us a ride home?" or "Can we take the El?" When they did win, there was always some kind of game. Once school was out, we were there all the time and sometimes took our friends.

My brother, being named Ron, Jr., got more pressure than I did playing baseball. I never felt that way in high school. I liked people knowing who my dad was, and I loved playing baseball. I wore number 10, I just wasn't as good as number 10. I was a decent ballplayer and when I got to college, it got a little more serious. I had a great high school coach who understood we were the sons of Ron Santo, and he nurtured that. You get with the wrong guy, and they don't nurture it, you're screwed.

When I got to college, the coach there didn't nurture that—he almost made an example out of me. I finally got to the point where I didn't want that. My dad said, "Screw it. Don't play." He didn't like seeing that. He didn't like that part of it so he stayed away a bit.

People don't realize that when you've got a famous father in the game, unless you are as good as he is, it's not easy. That's why you almost feel trapped. You've got to surpass your old man. That wasn't going to happen for Ronnie and me. At the same time, you still want to enjoy playing the game.

I haven't lived in Chicago for a long time. In L.A. I don't usually get asked about being kin to Ron Santo. I do get it from the random Cub fan I meet. They will always ask that, and that's cool when that happens. Santo is not a very common surname. It's funny because sometimes people who don't know call us S-a-n-t-o-s. Dad would always laugh about that. He'd hate it when someone would say, "That's Ron Santos." He would get fan mail and if any came in addressed to 'Santos' he would throw it in the garbage. "They don't know who I am."

Ron Santo was a cool dad. He was a dad who you feared at times. There's something cool about the discipline. It was tough because he was my dad...he was also this great ballplayer. Sometimes my dad's patience would run thin. He always cared about us. He was very overprotective. If anything happened to us, he wouldn't know what to do because he was so concerned for our well being.

One time, as a kid, I got hit by a line drive from Ernie Banks. Ronnie and I were shagging fly balls in left field in Scottsdale when they did spring training out there. Ronnie was catching them all so I tried to move in a little bit, playing deep short... which was a mistake. Ernie hit a frozen rope of a line drive. I had on one of Dad's old gloves that didn't really have a pocket with padding anymore. The line drive hit me square in the pocket of the glove, and broke two of the bones in my hand. I went down screaming and yelling. Fergie was standing by the bucket of balls in the outfield. He came and picked me up and ran me in— so I got hit by a Hall-of-Famer and picked up by a Hall-of-Famer. Fergie brought me to my dad, who was taking batting practice with Billy, and Ernie. My dad was so scared for me. I was crying. My hand was broken. When he grabbed me, it was like a tiger grabbing his cub. I was more in fear of the tiger than the injury anymore. He was shaking me. He was so scared for me. He ran me through the clubhouse and right across the street to a hospital. I was screaming for my life.

> One time, as a kid, I got hit by a line drive from Ernie Banks.

When I look back, I realize he was a caring father. He cared for us immensely. My sister was diagnosed recently with cancer, and that's all he cared about his last year—worrying about her. He was a great father. We have so many memories with him. We always found a way to laugh. He could be that tough, strict guy you just didn't want to see on his bad days. We also laughed a lot with him. Those were the extremes. That's my dad.

One extreme was when he had death threats. That was crazy. We had FBI guys 24 hours a day, protecting us. They followed our school buses to school. One time I got off at my friend's stop and they thought I was missing. They thought I got kidnapped. That scared the crap out of me. Dad would get these threats in the mail. It was right out of a *Hawaii Five-O* episode, I remember watching one of those episodes as a kid where this famous guy's son was kidnapped and the kidnappers would mail these cryptic letters that were written from magazine print. Dad was getting those same kind of letters. The FBI would open them up on our dining room table like a forensic team, dusting for prints, and these letters would be clipped in magazine print... "Ron Santo you will die on such and such day"... I was scared to be alone in public, every car that came close to me I would run thinking they were going to kidnap me. Then we would have these great dart gun fights with the FBI guys down in our basement. Ronnie and I had these top of the line dart guns in those days, and we'd build these forts in our basement. Ronnie shot one of the FBI guys right in the center of the forehead from about 20 feet away, hidden in a little sniper's chamber of furniture. The little suction dart stuck to the agent's forehead. It was hilarious. I remember they had an agent dress up like my dad to meet this nut case down at Wrigley Field one night. The guy had said he wouldn't send any more threats if my dad would meet him in person. So the agent goes down to Wrigley, at night, to meet this guy and he never showed. It was pretty serious that the Cubs even sent Dad home from **SHEA STADIUM*** thinking the guy was going to kill him there, that he was in the crowd.

The funeral was a very public presentation in a way, so we didn't grieve that much in Chicago. It was such a public situation. The funeral service was beautiful. My dad would have been blown away. The grieving process is tough, and I'd never gone through it, but you get it in different bouts. Yesterday would have been Dad's birthday so his passing really hit me hard on that day. I didn't even talk to anyone yesterday, which was probably the hardest day I've had. It's really strange now as baseball is starting. Keith Moreland has come in for Dad's

*During a 1979 New York Jets game at **SHEA STADIUM,** a remote control model airplane crashed into the stands at halftime, hit a Patriots fan and killed him.

position now, and that was sad for me. I'm happy for Keith—I'm just sad that Dad is no longer here.

I never looked at my dad as ever being old. He had that spirit, that strength about him. Even when I helped him out of bed that last night, he locked his hand with mine and I could still feel his strength, even that last night. He was a strong man. My dad was a strong, strong man.

Dad was naturally strong and was very gifted. I recently read an article that had come out in *Baseball Digest* in 1961 when he talked about meeting Mickey Mantle for the first time when he played in the 1958 Hearst All-Star Game in New York at **YANKEE STADIUM***. He was an 18-year-old kid and he noticed that Mickey Mantle's bat was so big. He wondered how he could swing that thing and hit the ball so far because he was not that big of a guy. If you looked at him, his wrist, his back, his hands were big. My dad was the same way. Those guys in that era were naturally strong and gifted ballplayers. Johnny Bench—same way. You shake their hands and it's like they've got an extra hand on there. They were naturally strong. They didn't work out. All their workout was running and actually playing baseball—that was their workout.

The idea for a documentary started when my dad went to the hospital for his second leg amputation. In 2001, they had tried to save the first leg with about 15 surgeries, where they started by taking off toes. They did skin grafts to hopefully heal the foot. They removed parts of his stomach that would be the blood source because, as a diabetic, you start to lose the flow of your blood in your feet, which is the first place to go because they are the farthest from the heart. The arteries down low on the leg start to deteriorate. They wanted to save the foot. It started

---

*The cement used to build **YANKEE STADIUM** was purchased from Thomas Edison who owned the huge Portland Cement Company.... Edison's middle name was Alva after the father of former Cleveland Indians owner Alva Bradley.

with a little sore on the bottom of his foot, which would not heal because he'd had diabetes for so long. When they tried to save that foot, he actually almost died. He went into cardiac arrest because the surgery took so long. They had to use the paddles to bring him back. Later he talked about having died and brought back to life, he said, "I didn't see a light. I don't know if that's a good thing." We laughed about that.

My sister and I went to Chicago to be there with him for the surgery. We didn't realize the operation was going to be so extensive that there would be these complications. He had decided to return to Arizona for the surgery to heal. We got to Arizona and realized that it was not working. He went through an unbelievable amount of surgeries. People don't realize what he survived...along, with having a bad heart at the same time.

In December of 2002, a year from the date of his operation to remove the first leg, he had his second leg removed. When he went in for the removal of his second leg, they told us they might be able to save the foot if they went in to try to remove the infection. We thought, "Oh no. Not this again." He asked, "If I get this operation done to remove the other leg, can I be walking by the first spring training game in 2003?" The doctor said, "I think you can." So, he said, "Take it off. I want to be walking by spring training."

I came in from L.A. and stayed with my mom in north Scottsdale. I would update her every time I came back from the hospital and she said to me "this would be an inspirational story to tell." The light bulb went off right there and we thought that it would be a great documentary film.

I had never done a documentary but I had done a feature before so I knew how to tell a story. I went to my dad the next day in the hospital and said, "Dad, I want to tell your story. I want to do a documentary film on you." He said, "Oh, son, I don't know about this." We talked for about two hours. He told me he didn't want to let me down by saying no, but he wasn't sure. I told him, "Dad, people need to know what you went through here. I'm your son, and I've seen how courageous all this has been. People need to see that. You can inspire millions of diabetics with your story. That's when he said, "All right, let's give it a try. I don't want anyone else or any other cameras in the hospital, just you. We'll give it a couple of weeks, and if it doesn't work out, we're not doing it."

During those couple of weeks, I was with him most of the time in the hospital helping him out so he was already used to me being there. He almost forgot about the camera being there 'cause I had already been there with him before we began. That's how it became so real. Those two weeks went by and he never said a word after that. He didn't tell me the two weeks were up and that he agreed or disagreed so we kept going. That's how it all started.

He'd be yelling at me because I would also be helping him at the same time. Obviously you get sick of one another because you are around each other for so long. That became a bit humorous. There is some humor in there where he got upset and looked at the camera and said, "Shut this thing off." I took it from that perspective and made it about him and his love affair with Chicago and dealing with diabetes and, while really battling this disease, accomplishing what he accomplished over the years. That was the focus. It wasn't about his personal life. It was really about the man—Ron Santo.

Thinking about the making of that movie now, I'm just so thankful for our time together. As a kid I was able to hang out with him at the ballpark and as an adult, because of *This Old Cub,* I got to hang out with him again. I got to be a part of his life as a broadcaster, I got to know all the guys in the radio booth, all the guys in the WGN truck, all the guys with the Cubs that traveled with him on the road. They were his second family, and for a period of time I was a part of that family.

The first time I showed it to the public was at the Cubs Convention in '04. I got a little nervous then wondering if that was the way we wanted to go out with it. John McDonough, Cubs Vice President at the time, is a real great marketing guy and he said, "This would be the best place to start this film." He had already seen a private screening of the film so I guess he had enough confidence in it to show it there.

If the baseball fans like it, it would be great, but if they don't, you're screwed. We get there on a Sunday and go to the ballroom, which had about 700 chairs set up. I have no clue what's going to happen so I'm a nervous wreck. My dad was so nervous that he left the Cubs Convention—he wouldn't stay for it. He took off early Sunday to go back to Arizona. I stayed and my producing partner, Tim Comstock, stayed.

It started filling up—so many people showed up that they had to put an additional 700 seats in there. There were so many people that it was standing room only—even the balconies were packed. I was standing in the back thinking, "This is crazy." I was worried about that many people seeing it and worrying about having technical problems.

When they showed it, I stood in the back, watching everybody. It was as quiet as could be in this room of 1500 people or so. I say to myself, "I think it's working. They like it." When the film ended, it received a 10-minute standing ovation. I was just blown up. I looked at Tim and said, "This is crazy, man." I didn't know what to think. I was so amazed by it all.

After it was all done, I had feelings I'd never had before. I called Dad, who was back in Arizona and said, "Dad, we showed it." He goes, "How did it go?" I told him there were 1500 people there who gave it a ten-minute standing ovation. He said, "You've got to be kidding me." I said, "No." He said, "Wow!"

I miss him so much.

SOMETIMES GOD JUST HANDS YOU ONE

LINDA SANTO BROWN

Ron Santo's youngest child, Linda, fought a major battle of her own with cancer beginning in 2010. She is currently doing well and living in Scottsdale, Arizona with her husband, David, and their two sons, Sam and Spencer.

My dad was out of baseball throughout my youth. I knew him as a businessman. I vaguely remember his last year with the White Sox. He was involved in my life more than you'd think. He even coached my softball team. Seeing my dad coach pre-adolescent, hormonal teenage girls was quite humorous. You put the two together and it really doesn't mix up well. There he was, though, coaching us from seventh grade through freshman year in high school. We played on an intramural Chicago bare-handed softball team and he coached us. We really intimidated the other teams with him because the other coaches knew who he was. So, we were a big draw. When we had our games, you'd think we were in the state finals just because Ron Santo was coaching us. He got himself into some trouble because he really irritated a couple of my friends. He didn't play them in the positions they wanted. He was all about strategy. I don't know about fairness. He really upset my one girlfriend because she wanted to pitch. It was a big game, he put her in right field and she couldn't pitch. When she walked away, under her breath she said "a------." Dad said "What did you call me?" He never forgot that. My poor friend, to this day, if I brought her name up he'd still be like—"Oh, I'm still mad at her—I don't like her"—just because of him remembering that.

We did make it, freshman year, to playing in the finals against a team of all seniors. Here we were these freshman girls playing these 18-year-olds who were not just your typical 18 year-old female athletes. They were like an East German team—huge softball players. They were fully grown—really big—and we were these puny little freshmen. We actually came within one run. That was when I really saw my dad's intensity on the field. He was screaming and yelling—in fact, the pitcher on the other team was a really tall girl and he was calling her "Daddy Longlegs." When I was up to bat he was yelling, "Don't let Daddy Longlegs intimidate you. Don't worry about Daddy Longlegs. Don't pay any attention to her." He was very serious. I just laugh because we were teenage girls playing 14-inch softball.

I went to Texas Christian University in Fort Worth. He would come down for parents' weekend. It was like the college he never went to. Before you'd know it, he had two fraternity houses entertaining him. I remember watching him across the parking lot carrying a case a beer over his shoulder with six fraternity guys. He was part of the fraternity. He would tell stories all weekend and have a crowd of 20 to 30 guys out at the TCU football tailgates just listening to baseball stories. They always looked forward to having him come to town. He'd take everyone to dinner. I'd get four or five of my guy friends and they'd just sit and listen to stories. He was one of them. Here we are in Texas and they still knew of him and loved him.

After TCU and Loyola-Chicago, I ended up having a career in radio advertising sales. I lived in downtown Chicago and spent a lot of days at Wrigley Field entertaining clients. It was great. It was a great advantage leaving Friday afternoons and taking my clients up to the booth and seeing Dad and then going to Bernie's afterwards—you know—making a day of it. Those were the best days. I'd sit front row at Wrigley, and Dad was worried that I was flirting with the players in the bullpen. He'd be staring at me with the binoculars and making sure that I wasn't talking to the players in the bullpen. I was there for four years and then decided to move out to Arizona in 1996. I bought a dog and a car and ended up working out here in radio. I didn't know anyone, except my parents, who were out here part time. Then shortly after I met my husband and started a family of my own. Arizona became my new home and having my dad here for six months made the transition seamless. Chicago never left us.

My husband Dave and I have two boys, Sam and Spencer. Sam is twelve and Spencer is six. My dad and Sam had a special bond because of their years together. We lived right next door to my dad for five of those years. Dad found the house and said he didn't want us to feel pressured to live there. As soon as Sam could walk, right after dinner, he'd say—"Can I go to Grandpa's?" and he go right over and watch TV with him until bedtime. They would have serious one-on-one UNO challenges that could last up to three hours as neither was willing to lose. They also would play a very competitive game of H.O.R.S.E. in trash basketball. Yes, trash basketball, this is where they would shoot a miniature basketball into a small waste basket. Eventually it switched to Nerf football with Sam versus Spencer and grandpa as the quarterback for both teams. It was great fun until something spilled or got broken— by grandpa, not the boys. We eventually built a gate between our houses. They were attached at the hip. When we moved it was hard—even though it was just a mile away. We cried. Most kids don't even live in the same town as their grandparents but you'd think we'd moved to Japan. We were so used to being next door and going back and forth. I am so grateful for those times.

Spencer was a sick baby and was in the ICU for two weeks. He showed his Santo spirit because he made it through when doctors didn't think he was going to. On my dad's first birthday after he passed, Spencer wanted to send a balloon off to heaven so that grandpa could read his note—he was very sad that day. He said, "It's not fair because I didn't get to spend enough time with him like Sam. He didn't get to know me well enough." I told him that "Grandpa loved you so much and held you as a baby." He said that didn't count because HE didn't remember him holding him as a baby. I told him, "Spencer, he laughed at you and loved all the time he spent with you. He's still watching over you." He then said he wishes he could get a ladder and climb up to heaven to see grandpa. We sent balloons that day. I'm sure Dad got the note.

Dad was more than a grandpa, he was his best friend, too. He would go over to Grandpa's and just hang out and watch movies. Dad would be here waiting after school when he'd get home off the bus. He would take him to get ice cream, get his hair cut, buy a new bat, a new Xbox game...grandpa was an easy sell for anything.

Dad would take Sam to the ballpark in spring training and Sam got to tag along when they were at Wrigley Field, so he was exposed to this other life outside of Arizona...he was blessed with this life but to him he was just grandpa...the rest was just a bonus. Once he got older he started to see how much grandpa meant as a Cub. He watched my dad with the fans, signing autographs, getting mobbed walking in and out of the ballpark, and shaking hands and laughing with players and coaches. It was at that time that I saw how much my dad meant to his fans and Chicago...seeing it through the eyes of my 9-year-old son. His expression said it all...he's not just any ol' grandpa.

> His expression said it all...he's not just any ol' grandpa.

My dad loved watching Sam play ball and tried to make every Little League game. He would watch him hit off a tee or take him to the batting cages...he even bought him his own hitting machine. Sam struggled with some confidence and grandpa would say "just have fun, just have fun. Don't think about it. Just go up and hit the ball. You're thinking too much." There was never any pressure from grandpa. It was just about having fun and loving the game. Little League opening night was this past Saturday and it was hard because it was his first game without grandpa. Sam had tryouts a few weeks prior and my brother, Jeff, took him. "I know it's hard without grandpa but you've got him cheering from above and he'll give you the strength." He went and did the tryout. I was texting my brother because I was nervous—I knew Sam could tense up and not do well in his tryout. One of the coaches, who's a well-known veteran coach, told Sam he wanted to pick him but he'd have to prove himself. Sam got that put in his face before the tryout. My brother texted me saying he was doing awesome. That coach ended up picking him. Sam came walking in with a big smile on his face. I asked what happened and he said, "I just had fun, Mom." First time he'd said it. They had him as a starting pitcher. We didn't even know he was a pitcher. On opening night, he struck out eight and pitched four scoreless innings, made unbelievable plays, got two hits—their team won 11-2... and he got the game ball. It was a packed game and people were coming up saying they couldn't believe that was Sam. I told them I think there is an angel in the outfield. I really do!

When I turned 40 I struggled with the feelings of getting old. When I was diagnosed with breast cancer in 2010, I thought I was way too young. I was blindsided by it. I was healthy and an active mom. My dad was always a hero to me in more ways than one. I admired and appreciated him for his fight off of the field. His fight against daily health issues and teaching strength and courage to so many people, especially in the Juvenile Diabetes community. He didn't have to go very far to teach this. Once again he was coaching me, but it wasn't on a softball field, it was on a much deeper level. He was my inspiration because of everything he'd gone through. I had strength but I also had some dark moments—some down times. He understood this. Through his words and actions, he taught me courage. Dad would call me and tell me—"Just don't think about it. I know what you're going through, and, honey, you're just like me. You're going to get through this and move forward. Don't think about it. Stay positive." I know it was hard for him to see me go through that. However, he just remained strong and steady for me. I had to really dig deep to see how my dad dealt with it. He was right. I am just like him. In the end, I came through because I tapped into that same spirit. I am now cancer-free and in full recovery—back to being an active mom.

I was looking so forward to getting him out here so we could all be together. It's always good to have him here in the off season. We spent almost every day together. I'd drive him to doctors' appointments and we loved buying wine and going out to dinner. When I was with him I always felt safe and secure and knew that everything was going to be okay. Even though I was 41 and a parent myself...I was always his little girl.

There are so many lasting memories of my dad: a lot of flash-backs of when we were younger and how much time we spent together, my birthday parties when he would give wild snow-mobile rides. And Christmases here were so important to him with the boys; and living next door and seeing him walk in through the back gate with an apple and a beer after doing a spring training game. He'd come and have a glass of red wine. We loved having red wine together. I still have a hard time going to a store called Total Wine by myself because I never went by myself. He always came with me. We never went there without him screaming and yelling at me because he was such a backseat driver. It's just a five-minute drive but it seemed liked twenty because he'd scream and yell that I was driving too fast; that I drove just like Vicki. I would get so tense when he was in the car. It got to the point where I would drive badly just because I knew he was watching me. He made me drive bad. Especially, if I made a wrong turn. He'd scream—"Why would you do this?" My son would just sit and laugh in the back seat but he would defend me, "Grandpa, she's driving fine." Dad would just yell, "Look at her. She's going 50 miles per hour!"

In the end Dad and I would end up laughing. We did that until October. In fact, I just had my last bottle of wine that we bought together.

He had such a gift of street smarts and business sense which was probably just experience. He was raised that way and he was a survivor. He was a self-taught man. Baseball broke him out of a poor childhood and then his spirit and will combined with street smarts got him to where he is. He was so humbled and honored by all of this. He would call me and say things like, "Honey, you should have seen the lines at Mesa, today. They were wrapped around and I signed for two hours straight." Or, he'd come back from a Cubs Convention and say the same things, "You should have seen it. They all stood up and applauded me. I think I got the largest standing ovation." He would be shocked by this.

My dad and I were very close. He was an amazing father and he loved life. I am so fortunate to have had him as long as I did. His presence and energy was so strong that there is this huge void left in our lives. It can never be filled and we will always feel it.

My dad and I talked about God and faith a lot, especially more recently—when you face health issues it becomes a more frequent topic. We always shared that special bond. There were times he had questions and I gave him my thoughts of certainty. Last year after I was diagnosed we went to church and prayed together. Later when we found out my successful results he came to me...he said, "I want to thank you...I'm just so happy you are going to be fine...I have no doubt my faith is stronger than ever and you helped me realize that." He was confident in this. He had faith. He taught me so much in life about courage, hope, and heart...he even taught me how to laugh at myself. I used to always thank him and tell him that I could never repay him for all that he had done for us. It felt good to finally give something back to a father who gave so much.

Chapter Three

LET'S SKEDADDLE TO SEATTLE

Growin' Up Ron Santo

SISTER KNOWS BEST

ADIELENE SANTO

Adielene Santo is Ron Santo's older sister and only sibling. She lives in Seattle.

Ron was a daredevil—never afraid of a thing. He spent a lot of time in the ER. My mother was the same way—she was never afraid of anything. My mother worked in the summer. I would take care of my brother 'cause I was two-and-a-half years older than he. Mother knew Ron, who was about eight at the time, could get out of hand and try things so she wanted me to watch over him

Every day, in the summer, Ron and I would go swimming—walk to the turnoff and go down to Mt. Baker Beach, where there would be a bunch of our friends. Ron had a habit of trying things. I'd be telling him, "You can't do this. Mom told you not to jump from this board to that board," or whatever. There was a fantastic diver who practiced there who was probably a senior in high school. All Ron could think about was this guy—because he wore a t-shirt, so did Ron.

As I was swimming, I turned around and saw Ron way up on the diving board. He does a big dive right off the board and somehow he let the board hit the back of his legs. Ron pops up from the water and starts complaining about his legs, he couldn't swim, so I start swimming as fast as I could to get to him. The lifeguard who was at the other end of the beach came down and asked if we were having trouble. I said, "No, my brother is just drowning." We pulled him in and took him up to the medical treatment area. We saw that his legs were just bruised.

Another time, Ron was trying to emulate the older, expert diver—Ron dove off trying a somersault and landed too flat—so that was another time we had to bring him up to the medics. Ron got to the point where he really turned out to be the most gorgeous diver.

One time we were all at Surprise Lake, which had the 50-foot board. Ron, at this time, was 11 years old. I told him not to go any higher than the ten board. He argued, "No, we can go to the 30. You've dove off the 20." I told him to definitely not do this because Mom would go bananas.

We were going up the wooden ladder. I told him the highest we would go would be the 30 and that I would go up first and he would go right after me. The structure started shaking and moving, and I got real nervous. I didn't even think about diving then—I just ran to the end of the board and jumped. I figured Ron would be right behind me. I didn't plan on him going on up to the 50. I came up from the water and looked up, and Ron yells, "Watch me." I thought I was going to die right there. He did a somersault—it was a jackknife and came off so beautifully that people on the beach clapped. It was unbelievable. I almost fainted because I thought our mother would kill me right now! He was that way. He had the guts and the grace.

He made All-City quarterback in football. My mother was always so worried about him getting hurt. He told her, "Mom, I'm going to get hurt if I have fear—I don't have it. I'll be fine. I'm going to make it. And he did. He was an All-City quarterback and he was fantastic. He had no fear of getting hurt at anything so he was good at it. My mother spent time hiding in a phone booth up at the stadium so she wouldn't embarrass him. She would pretend she was talking on the phone during football games because it made her so nervous to watch him play.

My biological father was an alcoholic. When he was sober, he was fantastic, and he was in the beginning. He drove for The Carnation Ice Cream Company. He's the one who taught Ron and me about sports. He was very, very good in sports—in everything. His drinking got so bad, though. It was hard on both of us. Ron and I wouldn't sleep at night waiting for him to come home, waiting for things to be all right. It was tough. Emotionally, it really drained Ron a lot. My mother was terrific. Her kids were the most important things in her life. We went through some bad years and she finally asked for a divorce while we were still in grade school. When she asked for a divorce, it was not the usual thing people did in those days.

Dad quit working for Carnation and got involved with my uncle who was in the restaurant business. Then, my dad went out on his own—into buying taverns and investing in them. That's when he got even more involved in his drinking. I don't know how much he owed or what he got because we never got into that. So, it came down to the fact that after Mom divorced my dad, Ron and I didn't see him a lot. My dad didn't give us any support—he skipped—he went out on a ship. He got out of town fast, just left us. Before this happened, my mother set up a time for us to meet with him. My grandfather would drive to drop us off, and my grandfather would wait with us for him... but my dad wouldn't show up. Afterward there would always be some excuse. It got to the point where Ron absolutely *did not want to see him.* ...and I didn't, either. Every time he called, he would be drunk.

After Ron was playing major league baseball, our dad did see Ron. Ron was in California and my dad then tried to get in with Ron. He waited for Ron to come out of the Dodger locker room and Ron talked to him, but he would have nothing to do with him. My father—NO—nothing—Ron would not have anything to do with him. My dad made a statement once that Ron wasn't going to be a ballplayer and he wouldn't be buying him good baseball shoes. But, my mom did everything to keep Ron in sports, and my grandfather was a great help also.

I had to deal with that a lot more than Ron did because when he went into baseball, my dad called me more. He didn't even try to get himself involved with Ron because Ron had told him, "This is it." Ron, in the end, did see my father before he died, and Ron took care of his funeral. My mother died in 1973 when I was 35 years old and Ron was 33. My father died after she did.

Ron was a very heavy tipper, but it's not because of him having any money or being a big baseball star or anything like that—it was because of how hard my mom had to work—she had two jobs working as a waitress. Because of my mother, my brother tipped high to all waitresses.

My mother was married a second time to my stepfather, John, for 20+ years. He was wonderful, and he and Ron became very close.

When my mom married John, Ron was in high school. He might as well have been our dad—he was that great. Larry, John's son, was younger than Ron and me when he came to live with us. The three of us used to get together and would be playing ball against the garage doors. We played quite a bit together. Larry was like a real brother. We never even thought of him as a stepbrother. Larry died at the age of 36 with congestive heart failure. It was really sad. He had rheumatic fever as a baby and evidently it weakened his heart.

It's hard to believe—given how tough and stoic Ron was as an adult—that he was a hypochondriac when he was young. For instance, one time it was polio season, and his legs went to sleep one night, he's yelling "Mom, Mom, I've got polio." Just stuff like that. He did a lot of crazy things. He had a great sense of humor. He was funny when he didn't even know he was funny.

He'd put this outfit on—he'd put that outfit on. As a young man, his hair had to be just right. He'd have these outfits laid out on beds. My mom ironed our clothes. She did everything. There would be creases in his Chinos or whatever he was wearing. He would stand at the mirror and yell at me asking how he looked. I said, "Ron, the last outfit looked good. Now, I'm not listening to you." He had to have everything just right, even as a young kid. He looked good when he went out, believe me. You never saw him any other way—even his jeans. He was a shoe man.

When Ron was 17, he was in great shape. He was always physically fit. Then, he started to lose weight. At the same time, he noticed things about himself like frequent urinating and extra fluids. He started drinking so much fluids—pop, water, everything. Mother never bought pop—she wanted us to drink milk. It got to the point where she was worried about him losing weight so she took him to a doctor who did the testing and found that he had diabetes. They also decided they would try a special pill on him, and with the diet and the pill, it was working.

When he signed to play ball, he decided he did not want anyone to know he had **DIABETES***. It was ten years before he said anything. The only reason he said something about it in ten years was because he wanted to give the opportunity to families who had kids suffering with diabetes knowledge that their kids could make the major leagues or do anything they wanted to get into.

When we all realized Ron would be getting a big bonus to sign, it was exciting for all of us. He had a lot of chances—Yankees, San Francisco wanted him as a catcher, Cincinnati. He was good at catcher, but he wanted third base real bad. The main thing Ron cared about was getting on a team where he would

---

*Other well known **DIABETICS** include: Jackie Robinson, Catfish Hunter, Bill Gullickson, Bears quarterback Jay Cutler, former Bears captain Mike Pyle and Bobby Clarke, the great hockey player.

be playing all the time. He thought he was going to get right in there...and he did.

In 1958, after his senior year, Ron went to Yankee Stadium to play in the Hearst All-Star game. He was going through it, down the halls—and he told me the thrill he had inside of him was unbelievable. He looked at all the pictures. He was thinking, "Oh, God, one day, I know I'm going to be on these walls." He didn't mean at Yankee Stadium...he just meant he would be on a team's wall. As he was going through the stadium, he went into the locker rooms and into another room where Mantle was on a table getting a rubdown. Ron saw him and immediately said to him, "**MICKEY MANTLE***!" "Yes?" Ron said, "I don't want to bother you right now, but I think you are so great." Mickey told him, "I'm busy right now getting this done." Ron starts to walk away. Mickey asked, "Who are you?" He told him who he was and Mantle said, "I never heard of you." Ron started walking a little bit more, he turned around and said to Mickey, "You will." When Ron had his first game in Pittsburgh, he got a telegram from Mickey Mantle. I don't know what happened to that, but I do know it happened.

I remember his call-up to the majors. It came at midnight, and mother answered the phone. I could hear her—they were bringing him up to the big leagues. The game was in Pittsburgh. He did so well. I asked him how he felt the first time up to bat. He said, "My knees started to shake so bad! I remembered those tennis balls against the garage. At first it was scary." But then after he got his first hit...it felt so good!

My mother did scrapbooks for Ron. Everything underneath these pictures were things he did throughout all of sports from the time he was little, all the way up to major league baseball. I do still have the scrapbook she kept for herself of her family

---

*Between walks and strikeouts, **MICKEY MANTLE** went the equivalent of seven full seasons without putting the bat on the ball.

and of Ron and me. Harry Caray, in his restaurant, as you walk in, has Ron's football picture as a quarterback. I don't know where they got that picture. Ron, Jr. wanted to take me over to look at it when I was there for the funeral. I told him that those were pictures that had been in our scrapbook.

Ron used to borrow my car all the time. My mom wanted me to let him use it. He never put any gas in the car. He'd run out of gas and John (dad) would have to pick him up. One time he let the battery go down and he had a girl in the car with him. That was my car. One Saturday after I washed it and it looked really good, Ron comes in asking if he can use my car. I told him, "No, get your friends to pick you up. Why is it always my car? You never put any gas in it." My mother comes in and says, "Oh, honey, if you're not using it, why don't you let him use it?" So...I let him use it.

On Sunday, my dad comes in from outside working in the yard. I was reading the paper and he says, "What happened to your car?"

I said, "What do you mean?"

"You've got a real big scratch on the hood of your car." John was good for kidding—I figured he wanted the couch.

I said, "You're not getting me off this couch."

He said, "I'm telling you right now that there's something wrong with your car."

My mother comes from the kitchen and says, "Now don't do that to her."

"I'm telling you. Come on out and see it."

I got up, and Mom and I go out.

There's a weird thing on the hood of my car like a white racing stripe—a white, wide, long, ugly scratch! It's not like he bumped into something. It was just weird.

I said, "Ron used my car last night. He did it."

Mother goes in and gets Ron up. Mind you, my brother, as a kid, could lie so well, but he couldn't fool me, but somehow he could fool mother. He puts a smirk on the side of his face, and we go out—the guy could have gotten an Academy Award. He walks over and says, "What's wrong?"

"Look at my car. That's what's wrong. What happened to it? You used it last night—what happened?"

"That was not me. I didn't do that."

My mother said, "What happened—did you back into something?"

I said, "How could he back into something to do that?"

He said, "Mom, I didn't do this."

She said to me, "Honey, something must have happened here, and we just don't know." I knew all along Ron had done this! Later, from his friend, I found out what happened.Larry and Ron were going down to the Drive-In to get a hamburger. There was a waitress there nicknamed "Betty Big Boobs." She should have been nicknamed "Betty Really Big Boobs." Where the trays are held on, there is a device that comes down from the overhang—Ron had rammed into that. He was looking at "Betty Big Boobs" and drove right into it.

Sunday night, March 18, 1973, after midnight, I got awakened by the telephone. I came up out of a deep sleep and thought it was someone calling me about work in the morning. I was groggy and said, "Hello." The caller said, "Adielene, this is your aunt." I said, "Who?" She repeated who she was. I looked at the clock. Then she said, "There's been an accident with your mom and dad." "An accident? Are they all right?" That's when she said they were gone.

I had lunch with my mother the day before they took off on the trip to Arizona for spring training. Ron had been with the Cubs for 13 years, yet Mom had never been to spring training. They were very excited about going and were meeting my aunt and uncle in Vegas. I was supposed to go on the trip with them. I was working for AT&T then, and I just missed out on the trip. I would never, ever have expected this. When John would take me some place in the car, he'd drive so slow, I'd have to tell him, "You've got to move." He would tell me to get out and walk.

There was a five-car accident. My folks went off of their route somehow. I don't know why my dad went out of their way on another road. They had changed the route on their trip and this happened to be one of those roads that had up and down hills. A semi somehow got involved, too. My folks and the truck driver, himself—the three of them died.

I jumped out of bed. Thank God I had a roommate. I was walking out in the hall saying, "They're gone. They're gone. They're gone." Some friends came. I was in a state of shock. I got downstairs. I called Ron at spring training. I told him what had happened. It wasn't good. Ron said, "I'm on my way." Larry, our other brother was on his way over. Judy got hold of him so he could get over to the house.

The three of us had to take care of everything. We had to set everything up. The bodies didn't get back until after they had done an autopsy, about a week. Ron and Judy stayed there with me. Also, Glenn Beckert asked Leo Durocher for a leave, and he said, "Go." He didn't have all of his clothes. He had got on the plane with Ron. Glenn and Ron were very, very close.

That was a terrible time. We worked together on everything. We had to get a huge church. It turned out to be the largest funeral they'd had. There were more than a thousand people there. They both had so many friends. We have so many relatives—it was huge. We two kids were everything to our mother. Ron had a very big bond with my mother. On every trip he made sure he would call my mother. The accident took a lot out of Ron—lots.

Mom's funeral was very, very tough for him. It's amazing how he held up with it. He was trying to hold me up as well...yet I wanted to try and hold him up, too. My mom used to always say, "There isn't anything that bad." And, after talking to her, we'd end up laughing. We are all programmed as we grow up—I remember my mother saying, "I'd rather have you single than unhappily married." Most of my girlfriends would say, "My mother can't wait for grandchildren. We've got to get married." My mother was not like that.

He and I talked about the Hall of Fame a lot. When his number was retired by the Cubs, he told me, "You know, Sis, I never thought that would ever happen." He told me about the whole thing—how it happened when he went into this office. He didn't know what he was going in for—he thought maybe his contract was going out with the broadcasting and the whole bit. He said he got in there, and it was a shock for him to learn that he was going to have his number retired. They don't usually retire a number unless you are in the Hall of Fame. He said that was everything to him and that even if he doesn't make the Hall of Fame, it was the appreciation for everything. Those Cub fans were everything to my brother.

I also coached Little League ball. Ron always told me, "Adielene, always tell me when someone from Seattle is coming to Chicago make sure you tell me." The father of one of the Little League kids was going to Chicago to be interviewed for a job. Ron got tickets for his family for a game and had a bat, glove and ball waiting there in the seats. He also had them come to the restaurant after the game and he went to their table. You can't believe my little guy coming and telling me this after he got home.

> Cub fans were everything to my brother.

Anybody who went to Chicago, Ron took care of everything. He always autographed balls for me when I went down there. I'd get a dozen balls, bring them home, and I'd give them out to charities here. Anytime I went with friends, he took care of everything.

Seven years in a row, six of us went to San Francisco, L.A. and San Diego to watch Ron in his playing days. I loved watching him play ball.

Ron's daughter, Linda, has gone through a lot. When I got a call from Ron in February, 2010, I see it listed on my caller ID. I wondered why he was calling me. I was planning to call him for his birthday but this was two weeks earlier. He said, "Adielene, your brother." I asked him, "What are you calling me for now?" He said, "Linda has breast cancer." I was just shocked. I've had breast cancer twice so he wanted to talk to me about it. He wouldn't talk to anybody else about this, not even Frank Savelli, his close friend, or anybody. Nobody knew anything—he just kept everything within the family. That's the way Ron was.

The biggest thing was his kids. Linda was seven years after Jeff. Ron and Linda were like two peas in a pod. He took her with him even as a baby—even took her to the ball field. Linda will tell you that Ron had to check out every guy who ever came calling. It hit Ron very, very hard when Linda was diagnosed with cancer.

I was with Ron in 2003 when he had his bladder out. When I got the call in late 2010 that Ron's bladder cancer had come back, I was so upset. What happened was the potassium, along with his second chemo, caused complications with the diabetes, and that's what he died from.

He told the family, "Don't call Ad until I find out for sure about this." He was so worried about telling me because then I would immediately fly down to Phoenix. He didn't want me to do that because he didn't think it was going to be that bad. He just felt that he was going to be okay.

At that point, Ron was feeling fine. He went in for a four-hour surgery, which got the defibrillator all set. That's where they found out that his lymph nodes were elevated, and they determined the cancer had spread into other areas. I didn't think my brother would do chemo. The doctors say that chemo with diabetes and especially bladder cancer is brutal. Ron told me that they told him that he only had six months if he didn't do the treatment, and that the treatment may make him quite ill. He thought he was strong enough to go through it.

He told me the only reason why he was doing chemo was because he wanted to have a little bit more time with the grandkids and with his kids. He said, "The doctors say that if I do this, there's a possibility I could maybe even live two years or a little longer." He was just getting ready to go to the ballgame his grandson was playing in. That was the last time I talked with him.

When we went to Chicago for the funeral and then up to Wrigley, I was shocked...shocked at how these cars would stop and people would be getting out on the street. I was flabbergasted. And then we got up to the ballpark and all those people were there. Ron, Jr. says, "I thought Addie was going to get out of the car and hug them all." I told him that if I could have, I would have.

Everyone who came into the wake was 'invitation only.' That was from 1:00 to 4:00. From 4:00 to 11:00, the fans were able to come in. Instead of me standing inside at the wake, I knew I would rather be out with the fans. I started to go out to the front. One of the security guys said, "I know you're Ron's sister. Are you going outside?" I told him I'd like to go out to see the fans who were standing outside the barricade. They said, "Great, but we're going to go out with you." I told them I'd be all right out there. They told me they had to do it. I told them it was okay but to stand a little bit behind me because I don't want to draw attention. I didn't even get all the way to the fans when a guy yelled out, "It's Ron's sister." I'm sure a lot of this had to do with the fact that Ron and I look alike, more now than when we were young.

I got out there and walked up to the people and told them that I was Ron's sister and I wanted particularly to be out there with them. I know my brother knew how much the fans cared for him, but I wanted them to know how much he cared for the fans." I told them, "Ron's kids are #1, and you guys are definitely—definitely #2!" I said, "He loved you, and I know he'd want me out here." They wanted my autograph, but I told them, "No. No. Please." They asked if they could take a picture. I went down the line with everybody.

When I got in to the wake and it was all done, we were supposed to go across the street to a reception—cocktail party. I said I was going to stay to be there when the fans come in. Ron, Jr. and Jeff said they were staying with me. We stayed there for about an hour and then went across the street. I know the fans appreciated it—they were so fantastic.

I don't know how this happened, but when I got home, I got fan mail. How they got my address was beyond me. Even my friends have a hard time figuring out my address, but they had my name spelled right, which they probably could have gotten out of the paper. How they got my address is unbelievable. The letters I got were beautiful—they were out of Park Ridge, Glenview—places where Ron had lived.

I've had a hard time since Ron passed. I had a partner for 25 years, and she passed in 2009. It was hard for me. I took care of her for six months until she passed away at home. She had two children, ages two and four, and I helped raise them—Christopher is 28—they are getting ready to have their first child, and Jill is 30 and she and her husband—they're having dogs!

I've got two of his big books with all of his pictures on my table here. The Cubs sent me the #10 that's on the 2011 Cubs uniforms. I put it on my desk. It's been hard. I told Jeff when he called me, "Every day still goes by...and it's still there...and I know it's going to be for a long while." I was given a neat, wonderful, loving brother...and I really miss him.

WHEN WE WERE YOUNG AND OUR WORLD WAS NEW

JUDY SANTO

Judy Santo was Ron's high school sweetheart. They married after his first year of pro ball and divorced after two decades. She lives in Scottsdale, Arizona.

Ron and I met in high school where he was a sophomore and I was a freshman. We started dating my sophomore year and dated throughout high school.

Ron was such a good athlete, and he loved to water ski. When he found out we had a speedboat, he'd have my brother take him water skiing all the time. Ron could get up on a five-foot piling—one foot on the piling, the other foot in the ski—and yell "hit it," and fly through the air and take off onto the water.

In high school, Ron played football, basketball and baseball. He was good at whatever he tried. Ron wasn't a great student, he lived to play sports. I remember one year he was failing algebra and the teacher made a deal with him—the teacher was a big football fan and said if Ron scored a touchdown and the team won, he'd give him a passing grade as long as Ron would never take a class from him again. Ron scored two touchdowns and they blew out the other team.

When Ron was first diagnosed with diabetes, the doctors didn't give him insulin—they tried to control it with diet and exercise. We went to some classes at a hospital in Seattle to learn about the disease. They were showing how to control it, how to give shots, and when we were there, a woman passed out from insulin reaction. This really scared Ron.

Ron realized that if he exercised before he took a blood sugar test, it would be low. Every time before we would go in, Ron would run up and down the hill to burn off the sugar. He was trying to not have to take the shot and wanted to avoid an insulin reaction. He was determined to be able to play baseball and thought that would be the way for him to handle it. After he came back from his first minor league season, Ron lost a lot of weight. The doctors told him if he didn't get on insulin, forget about even playing baseball, this could be fatal. So Ron agreed to take the insulin and figured out, on his own, how to balance his sugars while playing baseball. He would work himself so hard to see how far his sugars would drop, to where he's almost passing out—then he'd eat candy bars to see how fast his sugars would rise to where he was able to feel normal again. He did this for about a week straight until he knew exactly how to balance his insulin shots with the amount of food he ate to the amount of exercise he was going to endure. It was truly amazing how determined he was to not let this disease stop him from his dream of playing baseball.

At the end of his second year in the big leagues with the Cubs, Ron was awarded "Sophomore Player of the Year" from Major League Baseball. He had a great season and we wanted to buy a house so after that season Ron went in to meet with the Cubs General Manager, John Holland, to talk about his contract, to ask for a bonus. There weren't any agents then. So Ron walks in armed with all his statistics, 20 some home runs, 80 some RBI's, and so on. When Ron came out of that meeting it was like he would have paid them to play. John Holland had a comeback for everything said. Remember now, Ron was only twenty-one years old at the time. Ron felt like he had a horrible season after that meeting, it was like he was *Sophomore Failure of The Year*. I understand why these kids today have agents. If we had one, we would have definitely had a bigger house.

Back then, I would go to Wrigley Field with my son, Ronnie, and it was so empty, he would take his MatchBox® cars and play in the surrounding seats. Then Leo Durocher came along…and it was a whole new world.-

The Cubs players were a very close group of guys, but the wives were different. Back then, a lot of the families only came out during the summer when the kids weren't in school. They rented apartments instead of buying homes. But, we made our home in Chicago so we made local friends. We rented a house in Elmwood Park, that was predominantly an Italian neighborhood. A wonderful family who lived there, took us under their wing and became family. They watched over us and really helped us out. When we did things with them, like going out to dinner, things like that, we had our first introduction to the Chicago Syndicate. We went to a small restaurant, a syndicate hangout, where the food was great and we met people with names like "Catman", "Beanball", "Joey The Waiter", names like that.

When you're Italian, and you come from Seattle, you don't realize you're Italian. There's not the ethnicity out there. We were just all 'people.' When you move to a big city like Chicago, there are different pockets of nationalities. For an Italian boy to come to Chicago, with a big Italian presence, and live in Elmwood Park, a big Italian neighborhood, we were welcomed in. To start with, Ron's Uncle Sam had a friend in Chicago who was Italian and told him to help us. They lined us up with other Italian families. We went to certain affairs and became friends without knowing it. Come to find out, the FBI was out in front taking down license plate numbers and wrote down the license number of Ron's car. Ron would never do anything unethical. He was brought into the front office. They realized he was definitely not any part of it. It was just our being naïve and not even knowing what it was. So we had to stay away from social functions because we knew they were being watched. They seemed just like anyone else.

As the team began to play well, we hadn't realized we were *in a fish bowl*. We no longer had to wait in lines—we'd be moved right to the front of the line. If you got pulled over by the police, they would let you go, "Oh, you're Ron Santo." Those were how things were.

Ron grew to love Chicago. Everybody made him feel comfortable there.

There was nothing like '69 with the Bleacher Bums. Dick Selma, a pitcher who came off the bench, was bizarre. He'd get the crowd going. What enthusiasm he had. The whole year was incredible. We were so excited that *we were going to win this championship.* I went out and bought a roll-away bed for company we thought would come out and was planning to buy more, but then, the team started to slide. I remember Ron saying, "God was in New York that year." Each day, we kept thinking, "Okay, they're going to start winning again." And they didn't. Then, "Oh, they're going to win today." No! It was a very sickening feeling.

It was heartbreaking. He got so quiet. A lot of times, I couldn't even watch it on television because it hurt so much, especially when Ron was up to bat—it got so nerve-wracking.

The death threats started in Chicago. Whoever it was called into the Cubs and said he "was watching Ron Santo's family." Ron was out of town, but he immediately called in a panic. He wanted me to quickly get the kids inside the house. It was so surreal. Then, we had to have the FBI guard us 24-hours-a-day.

> The death threats started in Chicago.

I told Ron to have them come into the house, don't have them sit outside in their car. They'd end up sleeping on our couch at night. One time, I came down the stairs, and my foot hit the hallway floor loudly, and the guard jumped up. Startled, I thought "this guy's guarding us?" I remember Jeff and Ronnie talking about the dart games they played with them. Ron would invite them to go to dinner with us. We'd go to a local restaurant, with the FBI Agents, and treat them to dinner.

Ron had such emotions that you could really love him...or you could dislike him. He expressed himself. He put his whole heart into the game.

The Wrigley family would invite a few of us up to their home in Lake Geneva. They had this huge compound there, I remember we're all sitting at this large dining room table for lunch and they served us bologna sandwiches. Mary Beckert looked at me and said, "These are bologna sandwiches. " I said, "that's how they stay rich." The next time we got invited to the compound about ten of us went up there, even Joe Pepitone came up. That time they served two small roasted chickens for a party of ten—served on two trays by maids, two maids coming out of the swinging kitchen doors with two tiny chickens and lots and lots of corn. I guess they figured if the chickens don't last long there's plenty of corn to eat. We found out they grew the corn in the back acres of the compound. With all the crazy stuff that happened we always had lots and lots of laughs.

When Ron's parents were killed in the automobile accident, the call from Adielene came in the middle of the night. It was horrible. Two caskets going down the aisle. Two hearses going down to the cemetery. It was unbelievable. Right after, Ron went back to spring training. I guess there are different steps of healing. At first he seemed not to comprehend. But then, when he got to Chicago, it all came out in anger. He took it out on the baseball field. His batting average was unbelievable—close to .400. Then, the adjustment came along, and he came back down and started grieving. It was really sad.

Ron's mother had been told a long time ago that she would die in a plane crash. She was very reluctant to get on a plane. She agreed to a couple of times to come see us—one time it was to come to the All-Star Game in Washington D.C. Also, John liked to take his time and drive.

They were so good to my kids...they just knew how to love.

Ron's mother and stepfather had a wonderful relationship. They were beautiful people. Neither one of them could have survived without the other. That's about the only plus you could take away from the accident—they died together.

When we got married, we were two kids moving across the country to the big city. Our whole life changed. Over time, it all began to unravel. After our divorce, Ron had a good life...I had a good life. I'm not going to deny that the first two years, it was strained...but time is a great healer. But, always, *always*, Ron was so good with the kids. He made sure they had everything they needed. He spent time with them. Even at first when things were strained, he would make sure that I had what I needed. After that period of time, Ron and I became friends again. When I was diagnosed with multiple sclerosis, Ron would ask me, "Do you need anything?"

When he passed away, it was hard for me to take. My kids lost their father. And, I lost a friend.

I watched the funeral ceremony on the Internet here in Arizona. I was thinking that if Ron knew that all this was being done for him, he would be amazed at the tribute the Cubs and the City of Chicago gave to him. That kid from Garlic Gulch would never have believed it.

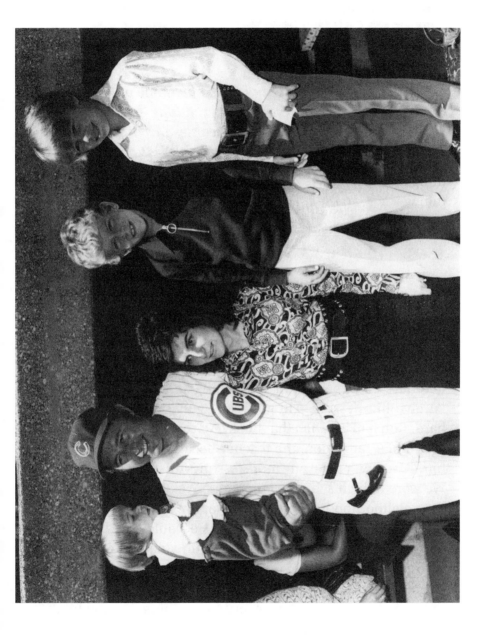

GROWIN' UP WITH RON SANTO WAS LIKE PLAYIN' HOOKY FROM LIFE

FRANK SAVELLI

Frank Savelli was one of Ron Santo's best friends, dating back to second grade in Seattle. Savelli is an estimator for a steel fabricating company in the Emerald City.

When I first met Ron we were both six years old going to St. Mary's grade school and we got into a fight. I was ten months older so I was a little bit tougher. We were going to show each other who was the toughest. So, as time went on, we continued to box. I was a good boxer. Ron felt that I could teach him something about it. We'd box and I'd give him lessons. He got really good and he hit awfully hard. Ron had a punch that Rocky Marciano would have been proud of. Pretty soon, the teacher became the student. I told him "You don't need any more lessons. This is getting painful." We were in high school by this time. We just boxed for fun in the neighborhood. I grew up in a family of pretty tough guys. Ron would have been a good boxer. He would have been good at whatever he did. God just made him a natural and he's so competitive. He'd get so mad if you did something wrong like not hustling. I was not a very good athlete but we used to play sandlot—baseball, football, every sport. This guy could hit the ball. I remember when he was a sophomore playing a game against Roosevelt. Their field was facing the school and the third level of the school didn't have screens on the windows.

He broke a couple of them. They put the screens in up there after that. He was just a great guy.

The only thing I was better at was bowling. He used to like to play the pinball machines and gamble a little bit. Every Sunday we would go to 5:00 Mass in the afternoon at the Cathedral. Afterwards, Ron and I would go down to this café where we'd play the pinball machines. One day, I told Ron "Why don't we just skip church." Oh, boy—he just looked at me like "skip church?" He said "I can't believe you said that!" So—we didn't skip church. I'd sit with him at church and when the basket came around, I'd put a dollar in and he'd nudge me like— that's not enough. I felt that was quite a bit in those days. But, I worked and he egged me on to put another buck in.

We went to the race track one day when we were about 16. We weren't old enough but we did a lot of things we weren't legally old enough to do. We were not old enough to play pinball machines, either. Ron always owed everybody money. He owed me money. He owed his sister money. He was always borrowing. He didn't have very much money—neither of us had very much. We won that day and when we were leaving the track, he said, "Don't tell anyone about this." I said, "Oh, Ron, for crying out loud. You've got the money. Pay your sister." Thank God I ripped the money he won on the pinball machines—$8. He was madder than hell. He left the bowling alley. I was bowling. I made $106 and he heard about it. He said "I knew you were going to come into the money after you took my eight bucks." That's nothing today.

Ron was a lover. He had girlfriends all the time. I doubled dated with him a few times. He was Casanova. He was a good-looking, blonde Swedish-Italian kid. Ron was a good dresser. Instead of having an open collar, John always made Ronnie button his collar. He looked pretty sharp doing that.

Another thing about him he was a hypochondriac. I used to tell him, "Ron, give it up." I'd sleep at his place. I was in one bed and he was in the other room. He had 20/20 vision. He had the greatest vision that God ever gave anybody. One day he was a little bit hazy and I went to pick him up. He was telling me that he had this and had that, that he was going blind, so he had to go in—there was always something wrong. He was a hypochondriac. When he was 18, he came up to the house and told me that he had diabetes, I pulled the same deal on him and said "C'mon. Don't give me that crap." But, this time he was right, unfortunately. He didn't want anyone to know because it would have hurt his career.

He was very close with his mother. I was very close to his mother, too. His parents were killed in an automobile accident going to spring training. She was really a nice lady. I wasn't a very good influence when we were young. She didn't want him to play with me. She said, "You hear the mouth on that kid?"

In sandlot games, I'd always choose Adielene instead of Ron. She was a real good athlete. We've been close friends all through school. She and Ron fought a lot. I pulled him off her a few times and said, "Don't ever hit your sister." She could handle it, though. It wasn't like she was losing that bad but I just told him it was the wrong thing to do.

I was always with him. I went with him everywhere he went. All his semi-pro games. We spent a week with his uncle, Sam Santo, who was a great person. He had a nightclub called The New Yorker in Tacoma. He would treat me and Ron like gold. Steak every night. Ron would fill up on salad and drive his uncle nuts. He liked salad but then he couldn't finish the steak. I never saw Ron's dad at all. He came to town a long time after Ron was into baseball for years. Ron told me his uncle wanted him to get together with him. Me and my wife and Judy were there, too. It was a cordial evening. Ron didn't have a lot of respect for his dad but he didn't deserve a lot of respect as I see it. I don't know where his dad was all those years. Ron didn't talk about his dad. He loved John, his step-dad. He was a nice person. We didn't do a lot of bad things—putting out streetlights and things like that with a BB gun. Ron got a bill for that.

When I would talk to Ron, he would always say he was fine. He'd never tell me about his surgery, but his sister would tell me. Whenever I called him, my message would say "You don't have to call me now—just call me at your convenience." He didn't like that. He'd always call me right back and say—"What do you mean, call you at my convenience? I resent that." Finally, at the end, I started to call him and I wasn't getting any callbacks. I couldn't believe he didn't call me. Ron can get annoyed and I thought maybe that I did something to annoy him. He finally called me but he still told me he was fine. It took a while, though, so I knew something had to be wrong. I called Adilene but she didn't know, either. She was down to Phoenix for some of the surgeries so she knew more than I knew, obviously. Anybody that goes through all that he went through—it's a miracle that he lasted as long as he did.

He was the best friend anybody could have ever had.

He was just a great friend. He was the best friend anybody could have ever had. I was blessed to grow up with him.

WHAT FRANKLIN HIGH SCHOOL NEEDS IS A FULLBACK, A HALFBACK ...AND RON SANTO BACK

BILL CHATALAS

Bill Chatalas was Ron Santo's class-mate in Seattle and teammate in football and basketball.

Ron Santo was a superb football player—the quarter-back, the punter, the safety. I'm not so sure if he kicked extra points or not. I don't remember if in those days we kicked extra points but if we did, he would have kicked them.

Ron was very intense and very tough. People would bounce right off him. If he needed two yards, he'd get two yards on a quarterback sneak. The guy could throw the ball the length of the football field. He really could. He had huge hands. He was a very accurate passer, as well.

Sometimes we'd get together, and he would never, ever forget this one play we did. I got hurt in the game before so I only played in one play. We were behind 7-6. It was in the middle of the fourth quarter, and we were on our own 30-yard line. I came in and we talked about the play. He said, "You go down 50 yards and I'll hit you." Fortunately, when I made my second cut, the defensive back turned his back on me. It made it easy for me to cut left and go downfield. This guy isn't within 20 yards of me. Ron hit me right on the numbers—50 yards down the field for a score. We ended up winning the game 13-7. Ron was good enough that he could have easily played big-time college football. **STANFORD*** really wanted him to be their quarterback. They wanted another John Brodie.

Our football coach was also the baseball coach. One day at practice, the coach is really irritated with us. He's having us do this play and that play over and over again. This went on and on, and the coach was just totally furious. Ronnie was really frustrated. He was frustrated because there was one kid who was being a dummy scrimmage star. The coach would tell the defense what the play was. The defense knew what the play was, but they were to play the play, not the ball. They were supposed to stay in their position. This one kid knew where the play was going every time, and he was always out of position and he was always where the ball was. Therefore, we kept screwing up because this guy was always in the middle of it. Ronnie got so frustrated he walked into the locker room, walked up to this guy and, with one punch, cold-cocked him.

He didn't look for trouble, but he didn't walk away from it either.

I didn't play baseball. He was a superb basketball player—tough. Ron was probably the toughest guy I ever knew in terms of intensity. We had a very small basketball team. Ronnie was a 6'1" forward. I was 5'10" and I was the tallest guard. He was always under the basket battling. He's up against guys 6'8" or 6'9". He always had a pretty good-sized body. He was well built even when he was a small freshman. In those days, I was lucky to be 145 pounds. He was an oversized kid for his age, and he was an excellent shooter. He was more of a scrapper. The only reason Ron was in school was because of sports. He

***STANFORD** quarterback John Elway signed a $100,000 bonus contract with the Yankees in 1981 and hit over .300 in his only year in pro baseball. His wide receiver Kenny Williams—now the General Manager of the White Sox—signed for a bonus of $125,000.

hated school. He was a smart guy, but he hated school. The only reason he was in school was to play sports. That's what was so funny about Stanford wanting him to play quarterback.

> **Ronnie was a very, very polite young guy.**

Ronnie was a very, very polite young guy. He never had a bad word to say about anybody. We hung together a lot because when I turned 16, I had a car and he didn't. He was usually with me. Most people thought that he was a cocky kid, but he really wasn't. I kept telling people that he wasn't cocky—he was just confident. He knew how good he was no matter what sport it was.

Ron was actually a bashful guy. His first date ever, he took his date on a bus. Three or four of us went back to Chicago two or three years ago. We were up in the booth there, and Pat Hughes, who also knows us very well, was there. Somehow we got a picture of this gal, and it was going back and forth between Pat Hughes and Ronnie and those of us in the booth. It was all about that first date he took on a city bus.

Ron and I double-dated a lot. One time we are out on a double date and I'm with a girl a year younger than me. He was with a gal who was even a year younger than her. The gal I'm out with lived up the street a couple of blocks from me. We were good friends. It was not a romantic type thing. A couple days, later, in the locker room, Ron asked me who that gal was I had been with. I told him. He said, "She's nice. I like her." I said, "Do you? Okay." So we switched...and he ended up marrying her. That was his first wife, Judy; the kids' mother. She was a great girl, a nice, nice person.

John Phillips, a lawyer and childhood friend, helped Ronnie out quite a bit after that automobile accident that killed his mother and dad. I didn't know this until John and I went back for the funeral. He told me, "When I was working on the accident, Ronnie wanted to nail the guy who caused the accident. He wanted me to try to find him." I don't think they ever found the guy who caused it. John told me, "If I found the guy, I would never have given his name to Ronnie." He was very upset about it.

Around our high school, the houses had alleys in the back. Nobody had garages in the front of their house. They were in the back, and the only way you could get to the garage was through an alley. There were a couple of alleys right where the high school was. The high school got complaints about so many kids going into those garages and smoking.

The principal came to Ronnie and me and asked us if we would do a "smoke patrol," and we would get credit for a class. We agreed to do that. Ronnie and I would go up and down these alleys. We would run into these kids who were out smoking. They said to us, "You aren't going to turn us in, are you?" Ronnie said, "Not if you give me your cigarettes." He probably would get 10 packs in an hour. So, he'd sit there and smoke cigarettes. We never did turn anybody in, but we would run them out. After Ronnie got their cigarettes, we'd tell them they had to go.

The house in Seattle—in an area called Garlic Gulch—where Ron grew up was right next to the baseball stadium. It was a residential—industrial area. It was a little tiny place. A guy named Dave Kosher, who was the Cubs scout who signed him, had cerebral palsy. He followed Ronnie around like a blanket. He would be at every basketball game, every football game and every baseball game that Ronnie played. Dave would come and hang out at their house. And at times he would even come up to my house to talk to me. He told me, "If I have to sign you, to get him, I'll do it." I said, "Dave, I've never played baseball." He said, "I don't care. You're fast. We'll teach you." I told him, "I don't think that's necessary, Dave." A lot of times, Dave would give Ronnie his car, and Dave would sit there with Ronnie's mother and stepfather for several hours. Ronnie would drive around, come up to my house and we'd run around. Can you imagine a college kid doing that now? The school would be on probation. Dave Kosher's dedication to Ron and the family might have influenced the stepfather, who was really the one to make the decision—not Ronnie." It was a very wise move.

After he signed the bonus contract in 1958, Ron went out and bought a new Chevy. It was funny. He went into the Chevrolet dealer right after he signed his contract. He had a t-shirt on. You know how guys used to put their cigarettes in the sleeve of their t-shirt—well, he was like that. He went into the dealership. He sees this Chevrolet convertible on the showroom floor. He opens the door and gets in and sits down in the driver's seat behind the steering wheel, like he was driving the car. The salesman comes over and says, "Hey, kid, what are you doing?" Ron says, "I'm looking at this car." The salesman said, "Get out of the car." He gets out of the car...and eventually drives the car out of the dealership. The guy thought he was some punk kid who didn't have any money. He plunks down two thousand five hundred dollars in one-hundred dollar bills and drives out of there with the car. He came over and took me for a drive.

Ron didn't play golf in high school. When he started playing major league baseball, he started playing golf. Before you know it, he's a 5-handicap. One time, when he had both prosthetic legs, he's working on his golf game. I asked him how he was doing. He said, "I can't hit a driver very well so I'm working on my 7-iron. It's teeing me off—I can only get 150 yards out of it." Here's a guy with no legs...he's hitting a 7-iron 150 yards...and in his 60s. I'm going, "You're complaining about that! I can't hit a 7-iron 150 yards, and I've got two legs."

I have never been to a funeral like Ron's. We were so glad that we went because it gave us a little bit of closure. We almost didn't go. Almost every time Ronnie and I talked, he'd tell me about a new bout with a medical problem. It was always one thing after the other. Almost every year, he was in the hospital two or three times. I asked him, "Ronnie, how many cats are you on?" He got a big kick out of that. It seemed like he had about 15 lives.

Chapter Four

A HARD WAY TO MAKE AN EASY LIVING

Baseball Friends

WE'RE GONNA GET TO THE BOTTOM OF THIS EVEN IF WE HAVE TO GO ALL THE WAY TO THE TOP

BUD SELIG

The Commissioner of Major League Baseball since 1992, Bud Selig and Ron Santo were good friends. He often joined "Pat & Ron" on the air on WGN during Cubs games, and he listened to their broadcasts often.

My daughter, Wendy Selig, adopted the Cub team after the **MILWAUKEE BRAVES*** left town in 1966, and just loved him. My mother was in Arizona in 1970 at a golf tournament and she saw Ron Santo. She said, "I gotta get Ron Santo's autograph." Mom goes up to Ron and says, "My granddaughter, Wendy, is a huge fan of yours." He takes off his cap, autographs it, "To Wendy, Ron Santo." She still has it to this day. That story tells you a lot because that's the kind of person Ron was. He was so good with people. He didn't know me at that time, and he didn't know Wendy.

---

*In the movie "Naked Gun" two prominent police officers were named Officer Adcock and Officer Mathews. The producers, David and Jerry Zucker loved Joe Adcock and Eddie Mathews when the Zuckers were growing up in **MILWAUKEE**. Eddie Mathews is the only **BRAVE** to play for the Boston, Milwaukee and Atlanta Braves....Plus he played minor league ball for the Braves in Milwaukee and Atlanta.

Back in the 40s, I was a Yankee fan but used to come to Wrigley Field all the time. My first trip to Wrigley was in 1945, the year they won the pennant. I really was a Cub fan a lot of years. When the Braves left, I would bring Wendy and my other daughter to Chicago often to see games. Ron Santo was a favorite of mine, as a matter of fact.

It was very exciting to go to Wrigley Field back in the forties and fifties. From Milwaukee, we'd take the old North Shore train down. Today, I get around to all the parks, but to this day, Wrigley's one of the few parks where I still get a thrill walking in. I get a rush of all those wonderful memories. I went the last Friday of 2010. I'm walking out on the field about 90 minutes before game time. I look over to the dugout bench and there's my pal, Ron Santo, sitting there. I went over and sat down, and we had the nicest long talk. I went on the air with him later on, which I always did when I went down. There was something about Ronnie I really took to right away. As the years went on, we became closer and closer. I really enjoyed our relationship...and I miss him. I'll be at a Cub game within the next two weeks, and I'll go in the booth with my friend Pat Hughes—he was here in Milwaukee for many years. I'll miss walking in and seeing Ron.

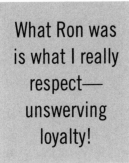

What Ron was is what I really respect— unswerving loyalty!

That day in the dugout, I sat with Ron for a good half hour and visited. In conversations with Ronnie, I always had a lot of questions for him. What do you think about this? He had great instincts and a great feel for the game, obviously.

There is no question that Ron Santo really loved the game of baseball. What Ron was is what I really respect—unswerving loyalty! He had a deep dedication to major league baseball and to his beloved Cubs. I loved that.

I always kidded him. I listened to all the Cub games. I'm 90 miles away, and they often play in the afternoon so I go to lunch and I'll have my radio on. I'll even continue listening to WGN when I get back to my office. I always say to him, "Hey, Ronnie. Let the play happen." Pat's describing it, and this voice in the background is groaning, 'Oh, no! Oh, no!' I already know what happened—it was bad. He liked that. He got a big kick out of that. He combined all the history—his great years there. He was so heroic when it came to his health. A lot of guys would complain and moan—I never heard Ron once. I'd call him at times after he'd had an operation and we'd talk. He's one of those people that I really feel privileged to have known. I have utmost respect and affection for him.

He was amazing. He loved being at the ballpark. I was stunned when I heard he had passed. I saw it on a crawl on one of the sports channels. I didn't have any idea he was in such bad shape. When I saw him that day in the dugout, I said, "Ronnie, I'll see you in Phoenix." Each of us has a home in Phoenix, and we'd occasionally bump into each other out there and talk. He said, "I'm looking forward to it. I can't wait to get there." I think Ron led a charmed life there at the end. We would call each other on occasion.

Speaking at Ron's funeral was a very emotional thing for me. I agonized. He embodies what you want in a person—loyalty, love of the game, understanding how important the game is and how it's bigger than all of us. He understood all that. He set a good example for this generation of players.

Wendy was also shocked when she heard he had died. It brought back a lot of memories. That cap story is really amazing when you think about it. He was playing golf *and he took his cap off!* The story is even more remarkable because he was very sensitive about taking his cap off.

There's no question I will miss Ron—I'll miss him every time I walk into the Cub broadcast booth. And, also, every time I turn on WGN, and he's not there. He always had a smile. There are not many of us who go through life not complaining...but Ron didn't.

PAPA BEAR

TOM RICKETTS

Ricketts grew up in Omaha and is the chairman of the Chicago Cubs. While attending the University of Chicago, he became a Cub fan during the memorable 1984 season, and he met his future wife Cecelia in the Wrigley Field bleachers. He and his siblings—sister Laura and brothers Pete and Todd—assumed ownership of the Cubs in Fall 2009.

My wife has an uncle who has had some health issues. We brought him to the park and took him on the field. We saw Ron sitting in the dugout. My wife's uncle is a huge Cubs fan—and a big Ron Santo fan. They sat and talked for a little while. So who pops out but Billy Williams. Billy and Ron started talking and somehow the old days came up. And, before you know it, they were just laughing and telling story after story about different ways that guys used to cheat in the 60's. They'd say, "Oh, yeah, then you'd throw the ball to second after a strikeout and then so and so would have that sandpaper in his glove." That wasn't atypical. That was kind of what happened before games with Ron. He just was there and he'd hang out and talk to everybody. Later that day, Ernie Banks came by where we were sitting, so her uncle got to meet all three of them in one day. It was an amazing thing.

Everyone was taken back. You have this impression that whether it's Hall of Famers or any type of celebrity that they're a little aloof or removed from regular folks. Ron was just the opposite. Anybody could walk right down and have a seat next to him in the dugout and the conversation began. He'd talk about anything that you would want to talk about and never got tired of talking with people and telling stories about his days or just talking baseball. He held court every day before the games.

The Cubs definitely made a conscious effort to do the funeral right. We wanted to just do it fitting of a Cub legend. It was interesting on the funeral side. The first day the visitation was from one o'clock in the afternoon until ten that night. From 1:00 to 4:00 was the family and friends which was nice. People were, obviously, sad but everyone was chatting and it was social. Everyone got in line and paid their respects to the family. At 4:00 when they let the first people who had been waiting in line all day, that's when it got sad. The people who came in were all just crying. They were much more emotional than even some of the family and friends because they'd been waiting all day and it was a big moment for them. Jeff and Ron, Jr. stood up in the front for a while greeting everybody. The people who had so much more emotion were a lot of the people who had never met him. It was just different. It was something that they will never forget—especially those people in line. Everyone was crying.

> He was one of these kids who listened to every single game on the radio.

There are those kinds of stories that come out of the funeral. There was a lady that had some kind of socially challenged young man who came to the wake that night. She came in and said, "Mr. Ricketts, can you get me tickets to the funeral tomorrow?" I said, "Of course. I'm sure we have some tickets for the funeral tomorrow." She said, "It's really important. The other day my son came in and said, 'My best friend just died.'" She said, "Your friend didn't die." And he said, "Yeah, my best friend died." He was talking about Ron. He was one of these kids who listened to every single game on the radio. There were lot of stories like that.

There were a handful of blind people who came. You forget what a radio means, sometimes. You sit and think and you see these people come to the wake. One thing that Pat does every game, he always goes through—in great detail—the uniforms of the teams, you know like "The **MARLINS*** are wearing their teal tops with the black pants with the teal and three stripe socks." We take for granted some things. It was just unbelievable.

I really wasn't surprised that Ron was so big in Chicago only because I know how much people love listening to the radio and love the WGN broadcast. On top of that, it wasn't like Ron was a wallflower and just around some of the time. He would do so many events. The JDRF people and the work he did for that is unbelievable. He was just tireless in terms of what he would do for the cause. You think about a player who hadn't played a game since 1974 so most the people coming through don't remember him as a player. I don't—or, just vaguely. Then you have all the people who knew him as a broadcaster for twenty years. Then you have all the people who knew him as someone who gave his time to work for the diabetes causes. It's a triple header. It was the way that he was a part of people lives. An amazing guy.

*The **MARLINS** are the only team that travels north to spring training…from Miami to Jupiter, Florida. The Marlins have never won their division, yet they have won two World Series.

RON SANTO WAS A HUMAN "RED BULL"

JOHN MCDONOUGH

McDonough is a Chicago native who was an executive in the Chicago Cubs front office for 25 years and worked with Ron Santo from 1990 to 2007. McDonough left his position as president of the Cubs in 2007 to assume the same position with the Chicago Blackhawks. In 2010, the Blackhawks won their first Stanley Cup in 49 years.

I had a chance to speak on behalf of the Cubs at his jersey retirement in 2003. I introduced the concept to the Cubs that we should retire his jersey because I had a sense—not that I'm generally right—that the Hall-of-Fame thing might not be imminent. Ron really was the ultimate Cub in many ways and had become almost the face of the franchise. And, a face of frustration. And, a face of everything. I was very proud of that and spoke on the field that day. I remember when the jersey was going up, the sun came out. It was a great day for everybody.

I miss Ron a lot. I saw him suffer a lot. The Cubs played a big, big, big role in his life. He would spill things. He would lose things. He'd forget things. He would lose his phone. He would just misplace things. I was very concerned about him in his later years—about him being on the road. I talked to him about just doing the home games. He didn't want to do that—he wanted to go out with his boots on. I thought at some point he would have come back and said that he would just do home games.

> He would believe that when they were 21 games out of first place they were going to get on a roll.

The Cubs were so vital to him. I really do believe he would go into spring training believing every year the Cubs would win the World Series. He would believe that when they were 21 games out of first place they were going to get on a roll—no doubt about it—and they were going to win the final 57 games and win the pennant and the World Series. I hoped for the same thing. He wished that so much and it was very painful for me to see him go through the Hall-of-Fame situation.

I was working for the Cubs when Ron Santo came back in 1990. Ron getting to work for the Cubs may have added ten years to his life...but, some of those Cub losses however may have cut a few years off. Working in the broadcast booth gave Ron, professionally, a real sense of purpose. He realized that he was a bigger celebrity as a broadcaster than he was as a player.

I introduced the concept of retiring Ron's jersey, "Don't we think it's time?" Then Cubs President Andy MacPhail played a role, as did Dennis FitzSimons from The Tribune Company. They bought in very quickly. When I told Ron—we were in a meeting with a roomful of other people, all hierarchy of the Cubs and Tribune Company—Ron thought he was getting fired. I said, "You know, Ron, sometimes these decisions are not easy to make. We wanted to make sure because of the nature of the subject matter, I just wanted to make sure there were other people here in the room." There was a really dark undertone to it. He thought he was getting fired. God knows for what? He thought he had done something. His face turned ashen. His head dropped a little bit, like *this is it.* I said, "I just wanted to let you know these decisions are never easy. This is my decision independently. This has been a tough decision for all of us. But we thought we'd come together and tell you that we're going to retire your number and we're going to raise your flag above Wrigley Field forever." I saw an emotional transformation I'd never really seen before in anybody—over a win, over anything. I saw someone's life change right before my eyes. I think the ultimate punctuation mark—the ultimate validation was when he said, "This is my Hall of Fame," I really do believe that it is. Just to have that jersey fly every day!

I'm sure he would look up there from the radio booth and give it five or ten seconds every day and realize that "this has been an amazing, amazing life in the place I love the most more than any place on Planet Earth. My jersey is retired and my flag flies about the stadium."

He was perfectly imperfect as an announcer. He would say to Pat Hughes when there'd be a runner on second base—remember this is radio, and he's the color announcer—"Pat, how did he get on?" He couldn't pronounce names.

People liked to tease him, and I think he loved being teased. The more mistakes Ron made and the more mispronunciations he made, the larger his legend grew. It told us that 162 games—3 ½ hours a day—you are going to make a lot of mistakes. This brings him down to that mortal state just like the rest of us. Some of the times it was funny. He would have no insight. There would be players who had played in the big leagues, like somebody from Atlanta, he would ask Pat, "When did they acquire him?" And it would have been that he had played for that team for eight or nine years. His homework was not preparation.

When you say the term 'winging it,' he personified that. That's why we loved him.

Even through these things, there was never any thought of firing him. He was so popular. **HARRY CARAY*** was a trailblazer for that. People loved the fact that it was not your traditional color analyst. It wasn't some homogenous presentation. I think they felt that here was a guy giving his heart and soul to this franchise, who lives and dies just like we do, we're going to give this guy a *lot* of latitude. And, we love him.

We did not judge Ron on his substance and content...we judged him on his emotional commitment. I don't know of any

---

*In the 1962 three-game playoff between the Giants and the Dodgers, **HARRY CARAY** did the local color on the San Francisco broadcast with Lon Simmons and Russ Hodges.

other broadcaster ever that you could say that about. It would be pretty hard for a play-by-play guy not to be. Pat might be the most precise broadcaster I've ever seen. He's brilliant. There was a nice ebb and flow between Pat and Ron.

The greatest compliment I ever received in my life—and I've been very fortunate in my career—and this is vintage Ron Santo—was when Ron said, "When I go into the Hall of Fame, I want you to be the one to introduce me." I was blown away— blown away. We had a very good relationship. There was strong mutual respect. I thought he felt that I had a pretty good handle on what I was doing. We socially bonded, as well. When Ron asked me to do that, to introduce him, was probably at a time when his Hall of Fame momentum was really gaining steam. We thought he was going to do it. I was so flattered, and then I realized they only do that in the **NFL***—they don't do that at Cooperstown when they induct someone into the Hall of Fame. But, just the thought that Ron would do this gesture—that he would invite me to introduce him to go into the Hall of Fame really was the apex of my baseball career.

In preparing for the funeral, I thought that the city of Chicago would come together...and it did. I thought this should be more a celebration of someone's life, as opposed to a wake or a funeral. This wouldn't be profound, devastating sadness— which it was, but it was a celebration. There was more laughter in that church and at the event afterward than for anyone I've ever seen before.

Ron seemed to live 25 lives. He kept on going...kept on going... kept on going! At some point, we thought he would be impervious to all of this. I was just happy that this didn't happen to him when he was on the road by himself in a hotel room. He needed a lot of care on the road.

*Politician Mitt Romney's full name is Willard Mitt Romney. Willard from J. W. Marriott's middle name...and Mitt from his relative Milton "Mitt" Romney, a former Chicago Bears quarterback.

THE HEART FULL DODGER

NED COLLETTI

A Chicago native who was both an avid Cubs fan and a huge Ron Santo fan. Now in his sixth season as the general manager of the Los Angeles Dodgers, he has also worked in the front offices of the Chicago Cubs and San Francisco Giants.

Growing up in Chicago in the vicinity of Franklin Park, I was a huge Cub fan. In 1964, I was ten years old. There was a little Italian delicatessen in our neighborhood called Al & Joe's. Ron Santo used to stop in there from time to time after home games to pick up some prosciutto, an Italian ham. Al and Joe, the guys who ran the store, knew I was a huge Cub fan, huge baseball fan, so they would start to tell me things like, "Ron called from the ballpark. He's going to stop here today." So I would ride my bike over there about three blocks and would wait for my hero to show up. He was so kind to me. I'd have a baseball question in some form, or I'd ask him to sign something. I might have had 30 Ron Santo autographs by the time I was fifteen. Even as a young kid who played Little League at that time, you knew that the guy who was spending a couple of minutes with you at the store was a star.

> I would ride my bike over there about three blocks and would wait for my hero to show up.

After a while, my family and all my friends believed me when I said I talked to Ron Santo because they began to tag along with me when I'd go to see him at the store. I might have six of my buddies with me by the time Santo got there.

When I got to be a teenager, I would go to the ballpark and sit in the bleachers. I would bring him some prosciutto from Al & Joe's, and once in a while, we'd talk. Sitting in the bleachers, you could always talk to the players. I'd tell a pitcher who was shagging in the outfield to tell Ronnie that Ned was there. After batting practice, Ronnie would run out, and I'd throw down the bag of prosciutto to him. When he stopped playing, we lost touch.

In 1990, when Ron got hired to begin broadcasting, I was in my eighth year with the Cubs. One day he called my office. He said, "Ned Colletti. Ned Colletti. That name. That's familiar to me." So I told him the story and he said, "That's incredible." He would come into my office that winter, and we would go over the team and the players and how the team was composed. I would explain "waivers" and "options" and "outrights" and all the vernacular of the game that a player from his era would not have worried about.

In spring training that year—1990—I found myself, in my mid-thirties, becoming a dear friend with someone I had idolized as a kid. We would spend days together, we traveled together and had dinners together. We chatted about the game after a game, analyzing the results. Ron always took losing harder than anybody on the bus. He loved the team so much and wanted it to be so successful that while anybody else would brush it off after a while, it always sat with him until the next game.

Ron was thrilled to get back to baseball after being away for a while. He almost couldn't believe his good fortune and the opportunity he was going to have to come back and be able to make a living and be part of baseball again.

Early in Ron's career, I was sitting in the booth with him in L.A. Frank Pulli was the umpire behind the plate. It was tough to find a place to sit so I would sit in the booth with them. I was next to Ronnie, and it's getting late in the game and the Dodgers knock down one of the Cub hitters. Frank Pulli goes out to the mound and he's telling the pitcher and is pointing to the dugout to say that both sides were being warned, "No more of this." On the air, Ronnie goes, "Well Pulli's going to stop this s--- right now." I looked at him, and he looked at me and I mouthed the word 's---' and he goes, "Oh my God!" I said, "Ronnie, you're lucky it's about midnight back in Chicago right now."

> "Oh my God!" I said, "Ronnie, you're lucky it's about midnight back in Chicago right now."

Maybe a year in, he told me that his popularity was then equal to what it was when he was a player. He says he's getting hundreds of requests every day for his autograph. I said, "That's great, Ronnie." He said, "I'm thinking about buying a stamp, and I'll just stamp the pictures and the baseballs and the cards and mail them back." I said, "You can't do that. You're who you are. You have to sign these things. You can't put a stamp on it and have a fan get a baseball back with a stamped signature on it." He totally agreed.

At this time, my son, Lou, is about 12 years old. He's been around the ballpark his whole life, and Ronnie knows him. I put Lou up to it—between innings of a game, he goes into the booth with a baseball and goes to Ron and says, "Mr. Santo, would you mind signing this for me?" Ronnie goes, "Absolutely." He grabs a ball and starts to write, "To Lou" and signing it on the sweet spot. Lou gives him this look and says, "Mr. Santo, I thought you were going to stamp it. I really don't want your autograph. I want the stamp." Ronnie looks up, finds me and says, "I can't believe you put him up to that."

In Philly there was a pay-per-view fight on after our game at Veterans Stadium. Thom Brennaman and Santo were going to stay after the game and watch the game on pay-per-view in the clubhouse. I go back to the hotel. Next day, I was going out to the ballpark on the bus. Brennaman was sitting across from me and Ronnie is in front of me. I said, "Hey, how was the fight last night?" Brennaman rolls his eyes and says, "I'll have to tell you later."

We get off the bus, and Brennaman grabs me and says, "Last night we get in a cab at Veterans Stadium. Ronnie gets in the front seat and says to the driver, "We're going to the Sheraton at Society Hill." The guy misunderstands Ronnie and takes him to a Sheraton in King of Prussia. They're driving and driving... Ronnie is getting hotter and hotter because he knows this is not the right way. The cab driver finally stops and Ronnie gets into it with him. He starts getting loud and said, "How stupid can you be? You don't even know where you're going. You're a cab driver in Philadelphia. We ask you a simple thing to do, and here we are out in the middle of nowhere." Everybody finally calms down and they go back and get dropped off at the right spot.

Tommy is telling me all this outside the bus as Ronnie walks in. Later that day, we're sitting around the cage. Ronnie doesn't know that I know what happened. I rather loudly tell Brennaman, "Did you guys see the paper this morning?" They both said "no." I said, "They've got this new law in Philadelphia so that the cab drivers can be protected. You can no longer not pay your bill and run out. You'll get fined heavily. You can't verbally or physically abuse anybody. You've got to keep quiet and if there's a problem, you report it professionally to a service, and they take care of it." Now, I'm making this whole thing up as I talk to Tommy! Ronnie is just standing there looking at me.

We leave, but the next day at the half of the third inning, I get the stadium operations guy at Veterans Stadium to let a policeman go into the booth. The guy has a piece of paper in his hand like a warrant, and he goes, "I'm looking for Mr. Ron Santo." Ronnie had his back to them. The broadcasters sit about four steps up from the bottom where the door is. Ronnie goes, "Yeah, that's me." And he turns around all chipper. He sees a policeman there and goes, "Yes?" The guy says, "Mr. Santo, did you happen to be in a cab at midnight two days ago?" "Yes, I was." "Did you tell the cab driver &^%# and *@#^*?" He goes, "Hey, wait a minute. I paid the cab. I paid him, but he didn't know where he was going." He gets really defensive. The policeman says, "Mr. Santo, we're going to have to take you in." Ron goes, "You can't take me in. I'm a broadcaster." He goes, "Sir, it doesn't matter. We have laws in this city." He grabs Ron's wrist and starts to put cuffs on him. Ron said, "You can't do this to me. I've got to be on the air." By now, they're back on the air. I peek around the corner...Ronnie looks at me. The policeman starts laughing. Ron goes, "I could just.... I could just...." Of course, by this time, they are back on the air.

The last time I saw Ron was the last time we played them, July 11, 2010. I made it a point always to stop in and see him and Pat. I would grab Ronnie for a couple of minutes and we'd talk about family and about baseball. He always told me how proud he was of me—I can't tell you what it meant to me, especially with my dad dying as a young man and me being without my dad through almost all my career. He would say every time, "Big Boy, I'm so proud of you." He'd almost have me in tears most of the time. I would always say to him, "Ronnie, my friend, I love you. You're one of my favorites forever!"

I went to the Dodgers in November of 2005. Outside of a couple of parking spaces reserved for ownership and the president of the club, I was told I could park wherever I wanted. The spots were all numbered. I park every day in spot #10. That started in 2005—not when he got sick or when he died—I did it right from the beginning....

MEET THE PREZ

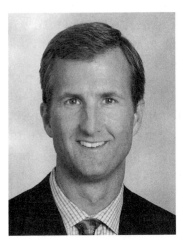

CRANE KENNEY

Crane Kenney has been president of the Chicago Cubs since the 2010 season. He founded Comcast Sportsnet Chicago, the Cubs cable partner, with Jerry Reinsdorf in 2003 and has served on the Board of Directors since its formation. Born in Quincy, MA, Kenney holds a law degree from the University of Michigan and a bachelors degree from the University of Notre Dame.

When we were at the ceremony at Hohokam Park on March 10, 2010 honoring Ron, I looked down the line of players lined up there. Obviously there were some fabulous players and some terrific athletes. I said about Ron, "I wonder how many of these folks realize how great a player Ron was. I don't know how many of those players would understand the magnitude of this player they were honoring, Ron Santo. They all aspire to be the best at their position. Here's a guy who truly was the best at his position and was recognized as such as a 9-time All Star. They probably have no idea that he spent 21 years in the radio booth and performed at such a level that he's not only a household name, but really considered part of the family for this massive audience. Here's a guy who, even after his playing career, built this incredible broadcast legacy for another 21 years. Then, in his spare time, taking on the cause that meant so much to him—Juvenile Diabetes. He raised $60,000,000 through all of his efforts with the JDRF walk and everything else he did.

I said to Pat Hughes, "As you look at these players, some would just hope to scratch the surface of his playing talent...and to go on to have either of the other two parts of his career would probably be a dream for any of them and here's a guy who did it all." We celebrated 50 years of Ron's life in baseball that day—a lifetime in baseball. What an incredible thing!

In our Cubs family, Ron was like the uncle, who always had a great story, could relate to everyone including the youngest intern who might have been intimidated to even speak to him all the way up to the most senior executive in the organization. Ron treated everyone the same. He was incredibly gracious with his time. You saw it with the fans. There wasn't a single fan I ever saw in 10 years that Ron didn't have time to talk to, wouldn't sign the autograph for. He turned no one away—fans, people inside the organization.

He was so giving of his time here. I can't imagine what was left at the end of the day, especially days with his illnesses. It had to wring the heck out of him. Like he did when he played...Ron left it all on the field, so, too, he left it all in the organization. We'll miss him for that. You can't replace him.

Keith Moreland, our new partner for Pat, has said it a few times on the air that he wasn't going to try to replace Ron because "No one can replace Ron." That's how everyone feels around here. Ron is really missed.

Chapter Five

HEY CHICAGO, WHADDAYA SAY?

The Fourth Estate Doesn't Take The Fifth

THE BLEACHER BUMS: WHERE BEER WAS MORE THAN A BREAKFAST DRINK

MIKE MURPHY

Murphy is a lifelong Cubs fan who attended his first game in 1958, and saw both Ernie Banks and Henry Aaron hit homers. He has been sitting in the Wrigley Field bleachers ever since. In 1967, Murphy met five other guys and that group grew into the "Left Field Bleacher Bums." He has performed as a long-time prominent Chicago sports talk radio host.

I met Ronnie in '61 when my father was president of the LaGrange Park Little League. Back then, the organization of about 150 kids would have a winter spaghetti banquet at a local restaurant and would actually have a ball player come and speak to the team. The fee was $100, which was a lot of money for our **LITTLE LEAGUE*** organization…and also a lot of money for a ballplayer.

Ron Santo was our guest speaker in '61. Since Dad was an officer in the league, I got to meet Ronnie before the banquet and got to talk to him a little bit after the banquet. From those days on, whenever I would go to a Cub game in the sixties—and, of course nobody went then—the paid attendance those days was 2-3-4,000 people, I always would wander down and stand around while they were doing batting practice. I'd yell, "Mike

Joey Jay and Ron Santo were the first two **LITTLE LEAGUERS to play major league baseball.*

Murphy from LaGrange Park Little League." Ron would always smile and say something like, "How you doing? How's your dad?" Ron was a great guy. Ronnie signed autographs every day before the game along the dugout and after walking to his car. I never, ever saw Ron turn down an autograph. I would have to say no one would have signed more autographs than Ron Santo. Ernie Banks was pretty good.

Ron was at my wedding. When I went to Ron's funeral here in Chicago, I was looking around the room at his children and his second wife, Vicki. I thought to myself, I might have known this guy longer than anybody in this room other than Ernie Banks and Billy Williams, who would have met him in spring training back in '59 and '60. Other than those two guys, I might be the third longest person knowing Ron Santo—albeit from age 10 at the Little League Banquet.

Ron paid attention to everybody. He was one of those guys who would sign autographs. And, again, not many people went to the ballgames. On a Sunday, a big crowd would be 15,000. I went to a Cub game in September of 1965 where the paid attendance was 538. I tell people I was at a game when there was 538 people there, and they can't believe it now.

In 1965, I was in eighth grade and was at a ballgame with a couple of thousand people there. I was sitting behind first base in what we used to call 'the grandstand,' the first row between the box seats and the rest of the ballpark. It was general admission.

As the game went on, I'm hearing this really loud whistle! I look around thinking it was some vendor. I keep looking around, and I realize it's only happening when the **PIRATES***— the opposition—were batting. I also noticed the whistle

---

*Forbes Field in Pittsburgh was so huge that the **PIRATES** would store the batting practice cage on the grass in distant center field....*The Pittsburgh Pirates was also the name of a National Hockey League team for five seasons in the 1920s.

happens when the Cub pitcher is winding up ready to throw. I finally realized that it was Santo. He did this whistle before every pitch as the Cub pitcher was winding up to throw his pitch. Like some people talk up the pitcher or the batter...I guess Ron's whistle was his 'talking it up.' It was amazing to me because then it pierced through the whole ballpark.

> He did this whistle before every pitch as the Cub pitcher was winding up to throw his pitch.

In later years, as the ballpark became more and more crowded, you couldn't hear the whistle anymore in the stands. By 1967, I couldn't hear the whistle anymore but I'm sure he was still doing it. That was one thing I always wanted to ask him about when I was with him, but I never thought of it at the time. I never thought of it until he passed.

I was talking to him once about when he first went to Double A ball, and he, along with three other Cub teammates, rented an apartment. They didn't have much money. One of his roommates was Ron Perranoski, a left-handed reliever later with the Dodgers and Twins. He was a Cub rookie who was traded to the Dodgers for Don Zimmer. The Cubs didn't think Santo was ready so they traded Perranoski for Zimmer to play third base in 1960. Within three months, Santo took his job. I always look back—Perranoski would have been on the '68-'69 Cubs and was the top lefty reliever in the business. Imagine if the Cubs had him in '69.

The Bleacher Bums were around '67-'71 and were basically high school and college guys. It was summer and most of us didn't have jobs because there was a recession at the time. We got to be famous because the press and the media found the 'Bleacher Bums.' We were the first group to take road trips. That sounds hard to fathom now. About 50 of us would rent a Greyhound bus and driver and would go to St. Louis to the old Busch Stadium, the big cookie-cutter bowl.

There would be 50,000 fans for the Cubs-Cardinals Fourth of July weekend series. It was hotter than hell. Nowadays you'd see 25,000 blue caps and you'd see 25,000 red caps. You see the same thing at Wrigley Field. About 20,000 Cardinal fans invade Chicago and fill the hotels and restaurants, which is a great economic boon.

I don't know why, but no one went to road games—not even all the Chicago fans in Springfield or Peoria and central Illinois. We would get the 50 Bleacher Bums down to St. Louis, and we'd be the only 50 Cubs fans there with 49,950 red-neck, hillbilly, crew-cut fans. We were all like long-hair hippies from the North. They were still fighting the Civil War down there.

We would get down there, and the Cardinal fans would pelt us and throw s--- at us the entire game. Wadded up beer cups—you name it. We would never wear Cubs baseball caps. If you look at the crowd pictures in '84, when **SANDBERG*** hit those home runs, you see very few people wearing team logos—t-shirts, jerseys, baseball caps. They weren't even sold or marketed by the MLB until after the mid-eighties.

The next time we went to St. Louis, we got yellow construction hard-hat helmets. Those became our trademark. But, we wore them for our safety.... Downtown St. Louis was a battleground ghetto. It had not been cleaned up then, but it's very nice now. As Bleacher Bums, we had no money—maybe ten bucks each in our pockets for the whole weekend. Tickets were a buck... but where would we stay? We would stay at the Cubs hotel on the west side of downtown, a beautiful 100-year-old hotel called the Chase Park Plaza. How we did this—to this day, I don't know. This was before you would make reservations over the Internet. One of our guys would clean up a little bit and

*Ryne **SANDBERG** came to the major leagues as a third baseman. The Cubs have employed over 100 third basemen since Ron Santo left after the 1973 season.

would get one or two rooms. We'd sleep 25 guys in each room. How we got through their security and their floor walkers and the house detectives—I don't know. We would take over this beautiful, opulent, classy, top-of-the-line American hotel. It had two or three bars—old-school saloon taverns, a beautiful lounge with a piano player.

> Ron pulls out a twenty dollar bill, throws it down and said, "Tonight, the Bums are drinking on me!"

We had no money...but we liked to drink beer. In '69, about 12-15 of us Bums were sitting at a table in this beautiful darkly-lit bar in this beautiful hotel. There was a piano player. There were wealthy St. Louis people hanging around at the bar. We're sitting there nursing a Busch beer. Ronnie comes in, and he sees us. We all know him, and he knows we're the Bleacher Bums who yell down at him and hang out. He walks over to us and asks how we're doing and laughs about the hotel security not throwing us out. He asks us what we're drinking, and we told him we were nursing a beer there. This doesn't sound like much today...but Ron pulls out a twenty dollar bill, throws it down and said, "Tonight, the Bums are drinking on me!" Probably back then the beers were thirty-five cents so we drank all night on Ron Santo. I'll never forget that as long as I live. That's the kind of guy Ron was.

Could you imagine a ballplayer today walking in, seeing some fans, and throwing down a couple of C-notes and saying "Tonight you're drinking on me."

We used to go to Ray's Bleacher Bar, now known as Murphy's—no relation to me. It would not be out of the ordinary that, after a ball game, Fergie and Ronnie would come in and have some beers. The utility players would come in—Dick Selma, Roberto Rodriguez.... Most of the players then were the same age as the bleacher bums—late teens to early twenties. Especially on the road, they would hang with us. It was a great relationship.

Forty thousand fans would go nuts when Ron did the 'clicking of the heels.' Normally, he would do it after a victory. Leo told him to do it. He did it impetuously that first time—happiness in the moment. It became a sore spot because other teams would use it as bulletin board material to rally against the Cubs. Nowadays, it would be reveled and glorified and everybody would love it. Back then, it was still old school—known then as 'showing up the opponent.'

Now if someone did that, it would be on the front page of **SPORTS ILLUSTRATED*** and every kid would do it...and every other team would do it. Back then, it wasn't done so Ron was either ahead of his time or other teams were looking for a mental advantage or bulletin board material. We loved it. Anyone who knew Ron knew that was just him. It wasn't like he sat down and planned for something to do to show up the other team. That's not Ronnie.

He was running down to the clubhouse. The Cubs had won in the ninth inning on a Jim Hickman homer, and the players had to run 200-300 feet to the old clubhouse under the stands by the left-field foul pole. ...so Ron clicks his heels a couple of times. What no one ever talks about is that here's a guy who was never known for gymnast-type moves, a pretty husky fellow for his height, to be able to gracefully make that move—to jump up in the air. He didn't click his heels just under his body—he clicked them way off to the side. When you think about that, it's almost like an optical illusion. It would be tough enough to jump straight up and click your heels underneath you. He clicked them like someone in Vaudeville—like Fred Astaire—it was amazing.

One time about '70, the Bleacher Bums were in Cincinnati on a road trip. Ronnie is in a terrible slump. We were staying in a hotel, the Netherland Hilton, which was the Cubs hotel there.

Who was the only Major League baseball player to grace the cover of the college football edition of **SPORTS ILLUSTRATED? Bo Jackson? No. Kirk Gibson? No. Rick Leach of Michigan? Yes.*

It was a beautiful, opulent hotel. Morning rolls around. There was a little coffee shop and I was there having coffee and toast, probably trying to get over a hangover from Bleacher Bum beer—that Cincinnati beer, Hudepohl and Weideman's. Our systems weren't used to Ohio River water beer. Santo was there and yelled out "Come here." I didn't want to bother him but I went over. He said, "There's something wrong with my swing." Here I was—a guy who had played high school baseball. There we were, right in the middle of a crowded restaurant at breakfast time. He grabs the table knife and he wrapped both hands around it like you would a baseball bat. Of course, the knife disappears in his two big ham-hock meat hands. He stood like he was taking his batting stance. Most of the people there were probably tourists passing through who didn't even know who he was, and they were all looking over at us. He says, "They're pitching me here. And then they're pitching me out there." He keeps moving back and forth. I was thinking, "What am I going to do?" He couldn't stop thinking about his slump. That's the way he was. He was one hundred percent baseball. I'd known the guy forever, but I was stunned. He was saying, "I'm doing something wrong." He wasn't really asking me for advice...he was just playing it through his mind, "What am I doing wrong?"

Ron loved people and loved signing autographs. He's very playful and loves practical jokes. My lovely wife, Dana and I were at a Cubs Convention about five years ago. There were long lines of people standing waiting to get autographs from **ERNIE BANKS***, Fergie Jenkins, Ron Santo. They announced that the autograph signings would end in 10-15 minutes. Dana and I were among the last ones in a long, straight line for Ron Santo's autograph. I told Dana we should stand close behind the people in front of us so Ron could not see our faces. We

---

*In the 1959 playoff against the Dodgers, Eddie Mathews hit his 46th home run of the season. That enabled him to win the home run title over Chicago's **ERNIE BANKS**, who finished with 45...and, of course, had no play-off games.

hunched down and turned a little to the side to stay hidden. We're the last ones in the line and when we get to the front, we keep our heads down so he doesn't really look at us to recognize us. I told Dana what to say when we got up to Ron. So, we get right up to him, and Dana says loudly, "Oh no. We thought this was the line for Fergie Jenkins." I'm still hunched down so he can't see me still. He turned beet red 'cause he has that short fuse. I pulled myself up and said, "Ron, we're just kidding you." He said, "Oh, you guys. You got me on that one. How are you?" And, he began hugging us.

There's one thing about Ron Santo. Everyone knows he's a nine-time All-Star, a five-time Gold Glover, 100 RBI's four times, 30 homers four years in a row—everyone knows his statistics. No one really mentions who the guy was as a player. No one ever talks about his on-base percentage.

The Hall-of-Fame thing was, to me, a travesty that he was not put in many years ago. Pull up his numbers sometime and look at his walks and on-base percentage year-by-year, and career. This guy would lead the league in walks and be in the top five in homers. This guy would be the league leader—or top five—on-base percentage. No one back then knew the phrase 'on-base percentage.' It had not been invented by Bill James and the Sabre-Matrician guys. Ron Santo was perennially in the top five-ten home run hitters, usually top five in the National League. He would be in the upper two or three in walks and on-base percentage. Plus, not just the five Gold Gloves, but they didn't have a thing called range factor then for fielding. But they did have a stat called 'chances.' In other words, how many assist-plus-putouts in a year. This guy led the league in chances nine years—range chances. So, the five Gold Gloves could have been nine. To have a guy who is a home-run hitter, leads the league in range and chances nine times, and was often the leader in walks and on-base percentage plus the power is a lock for the Hall of Fame. What happened was that no one talked about range or put-outs or chances back then. No one talked about walks or on-base percentage being important.

On my old radio show, when people—a Santo-hater, or a Sox fan, or a baseball fan—would say, "Well, if he hasn't been voted in yet, why would you vote him in now?" I'd say to them, "You know what. Here's why, in my opinion, Santo should still be voted in. There are new criteria nowadays. Bill James and the Society for American Baseball Research created this new criteria now to judge a player that didn't exist when he played. That's why you can argue about it." I don't hold water to the argument of "Well, if he didn't make it in the 80s or 90s, why would he make it now?"

He had tremendous **AT-BATS AGAINST HALL-OF-FAMERS***, actually, he did better against the Hall-of-Famers than he did against the other pitchers. That's a key. Then it was a four-man rotation. So, you go play the Dodgers—Koufax and Drysdale. So, 50 percent of your at-bats against the Dodgers were against Hall-of-Famers right there. Gaylord Perry and Juan Marichal—50 percent of your bats against the Giants were against Hall-of-Famers. These are amazing numbers.

Our wedding was in November, 1993, at a Catholic Church near Wrigley Field. We had our party and reception at the Stadium Club at Wrigley Field. We had 150-200 guests there. Ron Santo, Billy Williams and John McDonough were among our guests. My wife Dana had grown up in an Italian family in Chicago. Her Italian mother, of course, loved Ron Santo.

When Dana was in grade school in 1969, as did most kids in Chicago, she would get home from school in the afternoon and turn on the baseball game. Jack Brickhouse was our famous announcer. Dana's mom, Toni, loved Ron Santo. Obviously... Italian mom, Ron Santo—the star of the Cubs! Toni had a

*During his career, one out of every eight of Ron Santo's at-bats was against a HALL-OF-FAME pitcher

button made that said, "I love Ron Santo." She would put it on Dana's t-shirt or her cap. She wanted to make sure her daughter loved Ron Santo, which she did, along with all the great Italians in the family.

Going forward many years, that "I Love Ron Santo" button would always be around their house or up on the wall or someone would be wearing it. They took pride in that button. Then, the button gets put away after a while.

Dana's mom had never met Ron Santo, and she was more excited that he was going to be at the wedding and she would get to meet Ron than for the wedding itself. We get to the reception at the Stadium Club. There are tables, and the band is playing and Ron sat at a table with some of the Cubs people. We're trying to find a moment to bring Dana's mom over to meet him.

But...Dana has a better idea. She brought with her to the wedding that "I Love Ron Santo" button, Mom's old button from 1969. Mom didn't know Dana had it with her. We go over to where Ron was sitting at the dinner table and he greeted us. I told him I had to ask a favor. He said, "Anything. What?" I pointed out Dana's mom to him and told him she was his biggest fan and she couldn't wait to meet him. He said, "I'll go over to meet her." I told him what I wanted him to do. I showed him that old button—which looked old and home-made—and he looked at it and said, "What is this?" She was standing apart from us with her back to us so she didn't see us talking to him. I asked him to walk over and tap her on the shoulder and say, "Excuse me. Did you lose this button, ma'am?"

He's such a good sport, and he's so funny, and he loves things like that. He slips over behind her, taps her on her shoulder and holds out the button and says, "Excuse me, ma'am, did you lose this button?" She turns around...it's Ron Santo...she almost dies! She couldn't believe it was him—she hugged him. A lot of people wouldn't do something like that, but that was Ronnie.

THE WRITE GUY

FRED MITCHELL

A Chicago Tribune *sportswriter and columnist for 37 years, he was a record-setting place-kicker in college and became a member of the Wittenberg University Athletic Hall of Fame. A prestigious honor—The Fred Mitchell Award—is given annually to the nation's top collegiate place-kicker outside of Division I.*

Invariably there were some guys you looked up to as a kid and once you get to know them personally...they disappoint you because of their personality, and they turn out to be not the type of person you thought they were.

With Ron Santo, that certainly was not the case. To the very end, he was so accommodating, so personable that it was beyond what I expected. At least three times, I videotaped interviews with him. I'm especially happy now that I did that. I had Ron talk about his career and his life and his teammates—a variety of topics.

I had written a book with **BILLY WILLIAMS*** a couple of years ago. Billy and Ron's careers coincided to the point where they were teammates longer than any two players in major league history. I sat both of them down together in the dugout before a game. I videotaped that interview. It turned out to be a mutual admiration society. That particular interview with both of them sitting next to each other probably lasted 10 minutes. The two

Bob Gibson considered **BILLY WILLIAMS his toughest "out" and Sandy Koufax stated that former Cub, Gene Oliver, was his toughest "out."*

of them talked about the great times they had playing baseball. They also talked about what great friends they remained after their playing days were over. And about the fact that their families and their wives got along together so well.

It was a friendship that was born out of the fact they had played together for so many years. They both seemed to cherish that more than anything else. Billy told me that Ron bought a necklace and gave it to Billy's wife, Shirley. And, that she really appreciated it and always wears it. That's how close they were as friends.

They always batted 3-4, with Billy third and Ron fourth. Ron talked about how Billy was able to spit his gum or saliva out of his mouth and swing his bat and hit it while warming up in the on-deck circle. Ron said he would try to do the same thing and could never do it.

The eeriest interview I did with him was in June of 2010 at a Cubs/Sox game. He was talking about how hard he takes the Cub losses. At one point, he said, "I think the Cubs will kill me," something to that effect. He talked about wanting to come back for 2011. He knew that physically he wouldn't be able to handle all the traveling. He said the traveling had become really rough on him, and the doctors didn't advise it either. It was going to be toned down even more than it had been in recent years for him to continue doing it. He said that following the Cubs and doing that job was what he lived for.

> ...how Billy was able to spit his gum or saliva out of his mouth and swing his bat and hit it while warming up in the on-deck circle.

I was and I wasn't surprised when Ron passed. I know he had a strong will to carry on and follow the Cubs. His passion for baseball was way beyond any sort of a professional obligation. He loved the game, loved being around every aspect of it. I know it had to be difficult for him—mobility-wise to come down on the field and into the dugout into those tight quarters on a daily basis. And, yet he did it because he wanted to interview the manager in the dugout before the games and wanted to talk to players as they were coming out of the locker room and the dugout. He wanted to be a part of everything that was going on. I really admired that about him. It was similar to Harry Caray.

It's interesting how he gained iconic status...but it's neat that different generations of baseball fans got to know him. He would say later in his life that he became more popular as a broadcaster than he was as a player. I don't know if that's exactly true, but it could be. He distinguished himself in that manner. People were able to look past his shortcomings as a professional broadcaster because he had that self-deprecating humor about the type of job he did as a broadcaster. He always thought of himself as a baseball player first. After that he became a fan who just happened to be in the booth.

Ron had no pretense about being any type of a polished professional broadcaster. People appreciated the fact that he didn't take himself too seriously, which made him a unique asset in the radio booth.

RON SANTO MEMORIES ARE FREE... AND WORTH EVERY PENNY

DAVID KAPLAN

Kaplan worked with Ron Santo on numerous Cubs Radio pre-game shows the past 15 years. One of Chicago's busiest sportscasters, Kaplan is the long-time host of both WGN radio's Sports Central, *and Comcast TV's* Chicago Tribune Live. *The Chicago native is a die-hard Cub fan.*

I grew up wearing #10 in Little League because of Ron Santo. My hope was to get his autograph one day—the fact that I would be a colleague with him and a friend and play golf with him and go to dinner with him—that was beyond my wildest dreams. That would never even have crossed my mind. Then, in '95, I get hired at WGN, and I'm doing Cubs spring training ball games. Ron took me in immediately as a friend.

On my first Opening Day, 1995, I knew Thom Brennaman because I had done some college basketball games with him, and there's Ron Santo. I walked up to him and said, "Ron, I'm David Kaplan." He said, "I know exactly who you are. I've heard you on the radio before. Welcome to WGN. If you need anything, don't hesitate to ask." I said, "You were my favorite player growing up." I think he was blushing. He couldn't have been warmer, more welcoming. I'd do the pre-game show with Harry Caray and Ron Santo. Some of my most amazing memories in broadcasting—the reason I'm doing what I do for a living, without a doubt I try to pattern my style after Harry. Harry was the voice for fans. Harry was as honest as the day is long and Harry knew he was not broadcasting for the guy who owned the station. He was broadcasting for you in your car saying exactly what you were thinking about that team if they were playing well or playing, more often than not, not well. So, to work with Ron Santo and **HARRY CARAY*** ...

We were doing a game one night and his leg starts to bleed. He takes the prosthesis off. Dr. Adams, the Cubs' team doctor, comes up to the press box and checks him out. They get the bleeding stopped but can't get the leg back on because the stump is swollen. We help him from the booth after the game. He said to me, "I don't know how I'm going to get home. I can't drive without my leg." I said, "Ronnie, I live two minutes away from you. Here's what we'll do. I'll drive your truck home. A buddy of mine will drive my car and pick me up at your house." He said, "Oh God, that would be huge."

We get him down in the car, and I drive him home. Now, Ron Santo was my idol. He was my favorite player my whole life. He's got his one stump propped up on the dashboard. It has gauze on it, and it's bleeding. I looked at him and said, "Ronnie, I feel so bad for you." He looked at me and said, "Would you stop! We won tonight." I said, "Really?" He said, "Hey, it is what it is. I can't control it. As long as the ball club won, I had a good night." That was typical Ron Santo. The Cubs won...the world was an okay place, no matter what kind of personal stuff he was going through.

He's one of the funniest guys you'd have ever been around. The jokes that we played on him are legendary. One time, Ronnie was in the middle of the game at Wrigley Field about the sixth inning. I'm sitting right behind him, getting ready to do a

*In 1949, **HARRY CARAY**'s first wife Dorothy divorced him. In 1979 Harry wrote her: "Dearest Dorothy, Enclosed is my 360th alimony check. How much longer is this _ _ _ _ going to continue?" Dorothy responded: "Dearest Harry, Til death do us part. Love, Dorothy." Harry paid monthly till he passed away in Palm Springs in 1998.

scoreboard update on our broadcast. He takes his headset off. He twists around and looks at me like, "Oh my G--, my checkbook is laying in the parking lot downstairs." What made him think of this in the middle of the sixth inning—I have no idea. I said, "It's the sixth inning! Your checkbook's in the parking lot?" He said, "You've got to go down there right now. I dropped my checkbook in the parking lot. I just remembered it." I said, "Are you kidding?" He said, "I've got sixty grand in that account—they'll rob me blind." I said, "Okay." I take off my headset. I get his car keys. I run down and, of course, there's no checkbook in the parking lot. I open up the car...it's in his glove box, safely put away. Cubs vice-president, John McDonough sees me and asks me what I'm doing running down to Ronnie's car in the middle of the game. I said, "Ronnie thought he left his checkbook in the parking lot and wanted me to go get it." He said, "Was it there?" I said, "No, of course not. It was in his glove box."

> "Are you kidding?" He said, "I've got sixty grand in that account—they'll rob me blind."

Ron had asked me to bring it up to him when I found it. John and I decide to take one check out of the checkbook. We write it out to the Chicago Cubs Gift Store for $810.00. In the memo line, we write "Gifts for kids I met at ball park." We send a security guard up to the booth. I haven't gone back into the booth yet. John and I were hiding right around the corner where we could see the booth and hear what was said, but Ronnie can't see us. The security guard opens the door and goes in and said, "Ron, we just had some kids at the gift shop, and I wanted to bring you this copy for your tax records." He said, "What are you talking about?" I said, "This is for all those gifts you bought for those kids." Ron said, "I don't know what you're talking about." He hands Ron the copy of the check we had removed from the check book which said 'gift for kids.' This is while the game is going on. Ron said, "Oh my God. They've got my checkbook. They're going to take sixty thousand from me. I'm out of here."

As he gets to the door of the booth, he sees McDonough and I howling over by the lunchroom. He just looks at us, flips us off and goes back on the air.

The stuff we did to him...and the stuff he pulled on us was unbelievable. He was an easy target, but he would give it right back to you. He had that Italian temper. He was as good a person as you will ever, ever find.

He didn't have the greatest of relationships with Steve Stone. It is what it is. Ron and Stoney were not the best of friends, and that's fine—they were once traded for each other. Right before Opening Day one year, maybe 2001, Steve had missed a couple of seasons. He was out with an illness and left broadcasting for a little bit. They bring him back to throw out the first pitch. Now, we decide to play a joke on Ron.

We take a sheet of Cub stationery and write out PRESS RELEASE, just like when they had made a trade or got a new manager or signed a new player. It said, "Cubs announce expansion of radio booth. Former **CY YOUNG*** winner, Steve Stone, will join Pat Hughes at WGN Radio." It doesn't mention Santo at all—not a word. Then you read this long, legal-size sheet of paper. The entire press release said, "Pat and Steve will form the smartest booth in baseball. Our listeners will be better educated with Steve's great analysis," and, on and on and on—but, not a word about Ron. At the bottom of the release, we typed one line which said, "Former Cub infielder, Ron Santo, will also contribute to the broadcast." That's all it said.

Here comes Santo. I'm in McDonough's office with John, Jay Blunk and one other person. Here comes Ronnie. McDonough very casually said, "Hey, Ronnie, I just wanted you to see this release before we send it out." Ron was voice of the fans. He bristled because the characterization was that Steve was this

---

*As a young boy in Newcomerstown, Ohio, Woody Hayes was a batboy for a semi-pro baseball team managed by **CY YOUNG**.

brilliant analyst and here Ronnie was just this cheerleader. Ron's a brilliant baseball guy—knows the game as well as anybody. He then looks at this press release...Ron had come in and was in a good mood, it's Opening Day, and you see him getting redder and redder as he is reading this. I'll never forget it. I'm standing there watching the anger go up-up-up. He crumbles it up. He throws it at McDonough. Ron uses a bunch of four-letter words and says, "I quit." He walks out of the office, takes off down the hall and said, "I'm going to punch out the general manager of WGN Radio, and then I'm going home." We had to get to the end of the hall, and McDonough had to almost tackle him. It was one of the most hilarious things I've ever seen, but, Oh my God—it almost backfired!

In those days, I was 35 pounds heavier than I am right now. I am at the Cubs game sitting in the booth, most definitely chunky. It's now the fourth or fifth inning. I go in the press box food area, and get these awesome cheeseburgers. I get two of them on my plate with fries and bring it into the booth. The game is going on. Inning ends...Ron gets up to go get something to drink. Now, he's the most honest guy in the world. He stops, looks at this plate of food—he's always bad-mouthing me about my weight—he looks at me and goes, "Cripes, you need two more cheeseburgers after that lunch you ate?" I looked at him. He knew he had wounded me. I took the plate, dumped it in the garbage can right there, went on a diet that day...and lost 35 pounds. I worked out every day. I ate healthy. No doubt I credit Ronnie for that. When I would tell that story to Ron or around where he was, he'd go, "I never said that. I was never that harsh." Pat would look at him and go, "No, you actually were worse." There's absolutely no question that Ron was responsible for my losing all that weight.

When you heard Ronnie groan, that was exactly what the fan is doing at home. "What do you mean Derrek Lee hitting into another double play? Are you kidding?" That's exactly what the Cub fan feels when the guy doesn't come through in the ninth inning. Same deal.

AND MILES TO GO BEFORE WE WEEP

BRUCE MILES

Miles grew up watching Ron Santo in the 1960s and '70s. He has been a sportswriter covering baseball for The Daily Herald *since 1989, and has been the Chicago Cubs beat writer since 1998.*

I was born in '57 so I started watching baseball in the early 60s, WGN-Channel 9—Jack Brickhouse did both the Cubs and White Sox games. To me the best 3-4-5 hitters in the day were Williams, Santo and Banks in the middle of that order. That's what got me hooked on sports and baseball in wanting to become a writer or a broadcaster. I ended up in the newspaper business covering both the Cubs and the Sox. When I did Cubs games, I'd see Ronnie. It was like, "Wow, here's someone I cheered for and lived and died with as a kid when the Cubs won and lost and suffered the heartbreak of '69, and here I am working alongside him." Ronnie was so disarming. You never knew he was a superstar because he made you feel welcome. He made you feel important. He'd ask your opinion on things, ask your input on things, and always seemed to value it. There was no intimidation. Ronnie was so welcoming and so charming and disarming that way.

> You never knew he was a superstar because he made you feel welcome.

Ronnie was the most generous and genuine person I've ever met in baseball. I worked as a writer alongside Ronnie for 13 years when he was in the broadcast booth. He was the same guy off the air as he was on the air. Ron loved the Cubs. He lived and died with them.

Anytime you would go out, whether it was to a bar after a game or to a restaurant, with Ron, he insisted on buying. He would never, ever, ever let anybody buy a glass of wine, a glass of beer or dinner. He would get offended and would grab that check out of anyone's hand and say, "No, I am buying this."

The last couple of years our travel has been cut back a little bit at the *Daily Herald*, and Ronnie was very concerned about me and concerned about my well being. If I'd come on the road for a rare trip, I'd see Ronnie, and he'd say, "Big Boy. Are you all right? We needed you here. You have to get back on the road with us." The Cubs didn't need me, and nobody there needed me, but I felt like a million bucks every time Ronnie said that because he made me feel special.

One of the things I always liked to do the first day of a road trip was to go into the booth an hour or so before the game and sit with Pat and Ronnie. Ronnie was always interested in everybody's observations on the team. "So what do you think, Big Boy? Are we going to do it this year?" If you said to him, "No, I don't think we're looking too good," he would get offended. I remember back in 2001 one of the other writers did the pre-game show with Ronnie on the radio. Ronnie asked him if the team would win the division, and the guy said, "No." Ronnie said, "You hurt me by saying that." That really did hurt him. Ronnie wanted nothing but positives about the Cubs.

One of the greatest joys of the early part of spring training was hearing Ron Santo come into Fitch Park. You always heard him before you saw him because you heard everybody in the lobby jump up and say, "Hey, Ronnie's here." Then he'd walk in and he'd say, "Hey, Big Boy!" to everybody. He'd walk in and come into the press room and say, "How are we looking this year?" We'd tell him it was okay and they looked pretty good, "How do you think they look, Ronnie?" "Believe me! This is going to be our year!"

Whoever the manager was, whether it be Don Baylor or Dusty Baker or **LOU PINIELLA***, he'd say, "Where's Lou? Where's Dusty?" He'd get in that golf cart, and he'd drive around the camp giving everybody a pat on the back and tell them, "Hang in there, Big Boy. This is the year we do it."

Ronnie remained so popular with Cub fans in the booth because he expressed the emotions they were feeling at the time. When Brant Brown dropped that fly ball in Milwaukee, Cubs fans were thinking, "Oh, no," to themselves, but Ronnie blurted it out on the air, "OH, NO!" It was exactly what Cubs fans were feeling then. Ronnie expressed that every day— every single day. If the Cubs were going good, you knew it on the air by the spring in his step and in his voice. If Ronnie had that little bit of a lilt in his voice, and the smile in his voice, you knew the Cubs were winning. You automatically knew when you turned on the radio after a few seconds whether the Cubs were winning or losing because of the sound of Ronnie's voice. If you didn't hear Ronnie for minutes on end or if he was sighing, it was "OH, OH" the Cubs are losing today.

What struck me was that here was a guy in his life who carved out three very successful and distinct careers for himself. He was a baseball player...a successful businessman...and then he reinvented himself late in life as a successful broadcaster who related to the fans. Ernie Banks is always going to be Mr. Cub, no question about it. But, Ronnie achieved a standard quite near that of Ernie Banks simply because of his days on the radio. A lot of people who listen to the radio have no recollection of Ron Santo as a player, didn't know what he did after his playing career was over, but he was their companion every day on the radio. They

---

*When **LOU PINIELLA** played minor-league baseball in Aberdeen, South Dakota, the team's batboy was Cal Ripken Jr.

related to him so well that Ronnie became such a success in his third career to people who knew him only as a radio broadcaster.

It was the day he died. All of the news and all of the reaction came flooding in. I worked all day, until after eight that night, putting together stories and columns and remembrances and talking to people. I sat down and wrote the main obituary for our paper just because I knew him so well and knew his history. It seemed to flow. It's a piece I'm proud of because I wrote it from the heart. I wrote a column in spring training about Ronnie *not being there* and how sad it was. I wrote that from the heart also. It takes a while to get over that with somebody you grew close to over the years.

The only one I can remember whose death was treated in a like manner may have been Cardinal Bernadin, the very popular Archbishop of Chicago, who passed away some years ago. For a sports figure, I can't remember anyone else. I put on WGN television, WGN radio, all of it and it was non-stop. That, to me, was a measure of the man. He was a beloved baseball figure to be sure, but he was someone who gained tremendous popularity later in life.

I knew then that my work was cut out for me that day. I wanted to do it as a tribute to Ron and do the best I could on all my stories and my columns. The newspaper actually sent a photographer out to my house with a video camera, and I sat very studious looking in front of some bookshelves in my house and I talked for about five minutes, off the top of my head, about Ronnie, and we ran the video on our newspaper's website that day. That was among the many duties I had but it was nonstop that day. We talked about doing stories, about doing columns. Then, a couple of days later, for the Sunday paper I came back with the whole story about Ronnie's qualifications for the Hall-of-Fame, just thinking what a darn shame it was that he was never elected while he was alive to enjoy it. Those were all the things—the initial reaction to his death...writing his life story...writing a couple of remembrance columns...then, writing about the Hall of Fame over just the course of 12-14 hours.

A month later, we had a big planning meeting at the paper and I told my boss that one of the things I wanted to do was write a column about Ronnie not being at spring training and how strange it was going to seem. One of my favorite things was that on the first day when Ronnie showed up at spring training...you'd hear him. In 2011 it was quiet—too quiet for me! I wrote about him coming in and doing all the things I remembered—Ron walking in and everybody saying, "Hey, Ronnie's here." Ronnie would say, "Big Boy!" and "Believe me! This is going to be the year." Then he would go around and visit with everybody. It seemed so strange—just not right—too quiet that Ronnie was not there. I wanted to try to convey to the readers that—hey, while we're talking about the Cubs here, there's somebody very important who is missing. Spring training is not the same...and it's never going to be the same again!

Chapter Six

OF MIKES AND MEN

OH NO!!!!
Aw...Geez

CHOICE VOICE

THOM BRENNAMAN

Thom Brennaman was Ron Santo's WGN radio partner from 1990 to 1995. He is currently a Cincinnati Reds announcer, and a Fox TV NFL broadcaster. Brennaman has announced the BCS National Championship game three times.

In 1990, the three of us—Ron Santo, **BOB BRENLY***, and I—go to the audition down in Florida for the WGN job. I had already gotten the job, but they were trying to figure out who the analyst would be. The three of us went down together with Jack Rosenberg, a legendary figure at WGN. The four of us met there and had a chance to visit with each other the day before we were going to work—a walk-through of what we would be doing, what was expected. The four of us had dinner together and really hit it off. I had known Brenly relatively well before but did not know Ronnie at all. I'd never had any kind of contact with him because by the time I was old enough to know what was going on and my dad got the job in Cincinnati, Ronnie had retired. I never even got a chance to see him play.

During this interview, Ron was 'uncomfortable' nervous. We felt badly for him. Here I am a person in my twenties interviewing for a job. He was in his late forties, an accomplished former player who had done very well for himself in the

---

*Only four rookie managers have ever won a World Series, and only one has done it in the last 50 years—**BOB BRENLY**, with the 2001 Diamondbacks.

business world. Here he was in an interview for a job he very much wanted, and he was very nervous about it. He became even more nervous when he saw who the competition was. Anybody who follows the Cubs now would understand. It was extraordinary what a natural to broadcasting Bob Brenly was. He had just retired from playing three months before. He was part of the 1989 San Francisco Giants team. He walks into this audition, a polished big-league announcer *even though he has never done a game!*

Ronnie looks at Brenly and, as we start the audition, he realizes that if the competition is between the two of them, the only thing he has going in his favor is that he's Ron Santo of the Cubs. That's where it started and ended.

Because of the kind of guy Ronnie was—such a warm, open and engaging, loving and funny guy, when we got finished that first day, he looked me in the eye and said, "You know Thommy, I have no chance to get this job against Brenly." He and I were standing apart from Jack and Bobby. What am I going to say? I'm barely on the job for two weeks—I've never even done a game for the Cubs. I said, "Oh, come on. You never know what might happen."

What ended up happening was Jack Rosenberg was a very observing guy, and a guy who's been around a long time. Clearly the station preferred to have a former Cub in the booth, but they also wanted a big-league broadcast. Jack Rosenberg envisioned this all coming together with a three-man booth because we got along so well. We never would have got along so well if it weren't for Ron. Ronnie made it all happen. He's the reason we became a three-man booth.

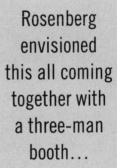

Rosenberg envisioned this all coming together with a three-man booth...

Rosenberg is a sharp guy. He saw how we got along, how we laughed, and how we bantered back and forth during that night we had dinner together and when we were hanging around each other away from those audition microphones. He ran the idea of a three-man booth by Dan Fabian, the WGN general manager at the time. Fabian went along with it and said, "Good idea. Let's try it."

We started working together at the spring training games. It was unbelievable that it was so much fun. I had never been to Arizona in my life. I get out there, and there's Ronnie, who had been to Arizona many, many times for spring training. He had a home out there. I'd like to tell you that he knew his way around the town, but I think I knew my way around better after about three weeks than he did!

He was always funny. We'd go play road games, and we'd jump in the car—and I say this with all the affection in the world when I use this term—and Ronnie always acts like the big shot when he thinks he knows something everybody else doesn't know. He'd get behind the wheel and start driving to Chandler or Scottsdale or Phoenix or wherever it was we would be going to broadcast a game. He would inevitably get lost. He would be having to turn around and would fly off the handle, cuss words flying in every direction. We went out all the time together for dinner or to have a beer. He wanted to show me all the places. I'd sit back and enjoy it all. They'd refer to me as 'the straw,' the one who would stir up conversations and topics, then would drop back and let things take their course. I'd put the ball on the tee, and Ronnie would take off. There were unbelievable great laughs and great times.

The very first day of Ron's first regular season broadcast, the three of us were also asked to throw out the ceremonial first pitch for the season at Wrigley Field. It's pouring down rain. The three of us went out to the mound, stood in the rain and threw the pitch. We hustled up to the booth and sat down, trying to catch our breath, getting one more sip of water, wind blowing, raining—game is going to be delayed, but we were still going on the air at 6:35, the scheduled time for the pre-game show.

Our engineer Don Albert used to say every day, "All right, boys, saddle up, here we go. 10-9...4-3-2-1." As I inhaled, getting ready to say, "It's a rainy night at Wrigley Field in Chicago—the first words to come out of my mouth, but what I hear loudly in my headset is "God d--- it!" I'm stunned. My eyes are looking around. I finally make eye contact with Santo and realize he's the one who said it. I look at him and a cup of steaming hot coffee has blown right into his lap all over his mid-section and his crotch. And that outburst was his reaction to this happening.

Here I was, 26 years old, my first day ever as a Cub broadcaster, hadn't yet said a word on air...and I'm thinking "my career has come to an end...because of this 50-year-old former Cub who shouldn't even be here to begin with." But, we plowed ahead. I went on with "It's a rainy night at Wrigley Field in Chicago. Welcome to Opening Day 1990." ...and off we went. Until Ron saw me turn and look at him, I don't think he had any idea that the mike was open and that he was going out over the air. But, he realized it immediately. Brenly was looking at me like he couldn't believe it either. Everybody was saying to himself a thousand things without saying anything. You just think it's over before it ever starts.

But it was always one of our favorite moments.

◇◇◇

On the air, or off the air, Ronnie was just like he would be if you met him in a grocery store, if you were lucky enough to be teamed up with him in a charity golf event, if you ran into him having a beer after a ball game at a hotel bar—no matter where you meet him, no matter when you're around him. Over the years, he's projected this as well as anybody I've ever heard or ever will hear. He was who he was...and who he was was just one warm, affectionate, loving guy. People know that. They weren't going to get wrapped up in how well he was analyzing the game.

They loved him because they just loved who he was.

WIT HAPPENS

BOB BRENLY

Bob Brenly worked with Ron Santo on Cubs Radio in 1990 and 1991. He played nine Major League seasons, all with San Francisco, except for 48 games with Toronto in 1989. Currently in his seventh year as color commentator on Cubs TV. He was born in Coshocton, Ohio and is a graduate of Ohio University.

Our first broadcast was opening day of 1990—Thom Brennaman was hired to be the new play-by-play voice and Ron Santo and I were co-analysts. As they were counting us down to airtime for our very first broadcast, you can blame it on the wind or blame it on Ron, but either way he knocked a cup of coffee over onto his scorecard. I've said many times, that might have been the last time Ron filled out a scorecard. The first words they heard from our new crew on the WGN radio were profanity. Ron, Thommy and I had spent a lot of time together in spring training that year—sometimes actually doing games from the booth and, on a couple of occasions, we just sat out on the grass berm with the fans and simulated calling a ballgame just so we could get used to each other's timing and sense of humor. Ron was new to the business, as was I. Thom was the voice of experience in the booth and he was leading us through some things. But, even in our practice games you could tell if Ron was a little frustrated because he was a baseball fan. He wasn't a broadcaster. He never had any illusions about being a radio broadcaster. He was a Cubs fan and even in those practice games when we sat out on that grass berm over at Hohokam or in Tempe—wherever—you could sense a little frustration from time to time from Ron. As I got to know him better, I knew he had a hair-trigger temper and unfortunately, we saw that right out of the chute on our very first broadcast.

We had all gone in for our interviews with WGN in Chicago and Jack Rosenberg came up with the idea that maybe to get some on-air tape of a ballgame, they would send us down to Florida for the, now defunct, Seniors League. The idea was that one day I would do the first five innings and Ron would do the last four, and the next day we would switch it. Jack would then come back to WGN with his recommendation and one of us was going to be the analyst for WGN radio. We got down to Florida and we hit it off. I had all the respect in the world for Ron Santo. I'd grown up watching, and reading and hearing about Ron Santo, and I knew his affection for the Cubs and their fans. Ron went into it thinking he had no chance. I felt the same way because certainly, WGN would want to have a former Cub in the booth and there was nobody more popular than Ron. So, I went down there thinking that I had no chance at the job. We'd do our thing every day. We would go out and have dinner and settle down over a few cocktails every night, and it was just a very enjoyable experience. It didn't feel like a competition, it just felt like a bunch of guys who really liked baseball sitting around and talking about the game and talking about the Cubs. From that interaction, after all our audition tapes, Jack Rosenberg said, "This could really work. You got a guy who recently retired off the field and who is very aware of the current players; you got a guy who has a bigger connection with the Cubs as any player in the history of the organization—why not hire them both?" Fortunately, for both of us, WGN took Jack's suggestion. It was a little crowded at times with three of us in what was usually a two-man booth, but I think more than the audition tapes, it was what Jack saw among the three of us sitting around a cocktail lounge in Florida late at night. I was very grateful. I didn't think I had a chance—I was happy just to go for the interview and make a tape so that I could use it in the future if I went for other jobs. Everything worked out so well and I'll be forever grateful to Jack Rosenberg.

This was all back when we were considerably younger and after a ballgame we used to like to go grab a bite to eat and have a few beers to calm down a little bit so that you could get to sleep after the game. We'd go out and have some cocktails once in a while. On one particular occasion, this is how I got a nickname for Ron Santo. I've called him "Chief" ever since I've known him. After quite a few cocktails one night, Ron informed me that he was part Native-American—that he had some Indian blood. I said, "Of course, if you're part Native American, I'm sure that you were the Chief." He laughed out loud a big belly laugh like Ron could do. That was it, I called him Chief every day after that every time I saw him. I don't know if he really did have Native American blood in him. I probably should have asked him the next day after we sobered up a little bit. But you come upon nicknames for people in odd ways. I don't know that anyone else knows that I had my pet name for Ron, but he always smiled when I called him Chief.

Ron lived in Arizona in the winter time and back when both of us played a lot more golf, we would play in a lot of the same charity tournaments. Of course, when he was still in the radio booth and I left to do TV in other places before returning to Chicago, our paths would cross several times over the course of the season. He was always good for a post-game "pop" somewhere and we'd tell a few war stories and catch up a little bit. Obviously, the last seven years he was working in Chicago, so I saw Ron pretty much every day except on those selected trips that he didn't make. That's been the hardest adjustment. I told Len on the air the other day that looking in that booth next door and not seeing Ron is like trying to play a baseball game without first base. Something just seems to be missing and I don't know how long it's going to take to get over that.

IF YOU'RE LUCKY ENOUGH
TO WORK WITH RON SANTO,
YOU'RE LUCKY ENOUGH

LEN KASPER

A Michigan native, Kasper is a ten-year veteran of broadcasting Major League baseball. After a three-year stint as the television play-by-play voice of the Florida Marlins, he is currently in his seventh season as the Chicago Cubs TV play-by-play voice.

We would do West Coast trips where we would play in Arizona, and then fly into San Francisco and get in about 2:30 a.m. San Francisco time, which is 4:30 a.m. Chicago time, and we'd all be worn out. I was in my mid-to-late thirties at the time, and Ron was in his sixties—a diabetic, no legs, and you'd see him get off the bus. You say to yourself I don't know how I do it, and you'd look at Ron and say how can he do it? You learned not to complain because you realized how much he had to go through every day just to get out of bed and go to the ballpark.

Just as former player **TIM MCCARVER*** will be remembered as a broadcaster, Ron Santo will be remembered as a fan/broadcaster/player all wrapped into one. It's almost like he defies description. He took his broadcasting career very seriously. I take umbrage with anybody who says that Ron did not prepare.

---

*Brent Musburger was the home plate umpire when **TIM MCCARVER** made his pro baseball debut for Keokuk, Iowa, in the Midwest League in 1959.

That's not true. I spent a lot of time with him in the manager's office, the clubhouse and the dugout. He always wanted to know what was going on in that clubhouse. Did he pore through media guides like play-by-play announcers do and find biographical information? No. But, that's not what Ron was supposed to do. Ron was a Cub, and he spent an hour in the manager's office every day and in the coaches' room. He asked a lot of questions. He was very prepared when it came to the Chicago Cubs every day. When I hear people say that he didn't know what he was talking about—it's just not true. He sometimes had issues in conveying what he knew and sometimes he'd get lost in thought and that's what made it fun. He'd poke fun of himself... but, he knew the Cubs. He knew what was going on on a daily basis.

> He'd poke fun of himself...but, he knew the Cubs. He knew what was going on on a daily basis.

The last year, it was actually a pretty serious thing—he cut himself shaving right above his upper lip. It was bleeding all day and he could not stop it. Fortunately, it was ultimately okay, but before the game one of the Cub doctors walked in to try to stop the bleeding. They put some gauze and some white masking tape over his upper lip. It looked funny...and Ron knew it looked funny. Somebody in the radio booth tipped us off that Ron had this white mustache look. We showed it, and we asked, "Hey, what's going on with Ron today?" "I think he cut his lip." He was laughing as we were showing him. We go to break, and, during the break, we got some white masking tape, and as we come out of break, Bob and I both have the white masking tape on—matching what Ron had on. He thought that was the funniest thing ever. Those are the moments where we really felt we bonded with him. You were having fun with him. You weren't making fun of his situation. I found out later that he was bleeding all day. I don't know if he may have been on some kind of blood thinner or something. He had fun with it and, to him, those kinds of things were no big deal. If I had a cut and it bled for three or four hours, I'd be freaking out. But, because he handled all the things health-wise that he did over the course of his life, those things were just, "Eeeh, we'll fix it, and it'll be fine." He was able to poke fun at himself.

Ron Santo had passed on Thursday night. I was called before six in the morning on Friday. I did not realize the end was so near. He'd had a rough season in that he had to take some trips off that previously he would have battled his way through. In that regard, I knew it was a tough year. I did not know about the bladder cancer, which ultimately led to his death.

Ron would have a heart procedure. You would ask him how it was going. He'd be like yeah, it was a little heart thing. "What?" "Oh, they just went in and put a stent in or whatever." "You're kidding!" "I'm fine." It would be like us having a cold. Things didn't faze him.

I will miss hanging in the manager's office with Ron, which I did every day during the season. The years we had with Lou Piniella, in particular, were days I will cherish. Just sitting in Lou's office, with Lou and Ron, reminiscing. Hearing Ron ask Lou about his Yankee days and Lou bringing up a player from the sixties that Ron played against, a pitcher he faced. They would tell story after story after story. Then we'd talk about the day's news. We'd talk about the team. I'd ask them questions, and they'd ask me a question. I was so honored to just be able to sit in that room and talk to two baseball giants every day.

THE BRADY PUNCH

MARC BRADY

Brady, a Chicago native, is a Columbia College graduate who has worked at WGN-TV since 1998. After serving as Associate Producer for eleven years, he is currently in his third season as Producer for WGN-TV on Chicago Cubs telecasts. A five-time Emmy award winner, Brady is also in his third year producing Chicago Blackhawks games on WGN-TV.

In 2007, we were at Cincinnati, in a lobby that was full of Cub fans. We clinched on a Friday night so none of the starters are going to play on Saturday. Most times the team bus is reserved for players who are injured, or guys who knew they were not going to play, and the broadcasters—Ron Santo, Pat Hughes, Len Kasper and Bob Brenly. The day after they clinched, the team bus was populated with some of the bigger players who would not usually be riding that bus. As I come down to the lobby, I noticed Derrek Lee, Aramis Ramirez and a few other guys are all walking ahead of Ron Santo and me. The fans are all running toward the players. The closer Santo gets to the crowd of people, the fans break away from the players who had just won the Division the night before and run over to Santo to get his autograph. The man would never say "No" to anyone, so I'm holding his bag. I stood with him at least 10 minutes, and then I walked away from him, got on the bus and waited for him there. It was amazing to watch. That many people who had just watched their heroes win the Division...ran away from their heroes to go see Ron Santo. We sat on the bus and watched it all and laughed as he signed for everyone.

At one time in Miami, it always seemed like there was more security than actual fans. The games would have an attendance of 300-400 people but yet there would be 300-400 security guys. We were coming off the bus. There aren't usually many people checking to see what was going on as we came off the bus. Ron never wore a media pass. *Ron didn't need to wear a media pass...he's Ron Santo!* As we all walked off the bus, they were checking for our passes. When Ron gets to them, they ask where his pass is. Ron said, "I don't have a pass." "Well, sir, why don't you have a media pass?" Ron said, "BECAUSE I'M NOT MEDIA." The man said, "Then, what are you?" Ron said, "I'm a baseball player." As he stands there with his artificial legs.

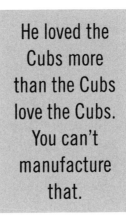

He loved the Cubs more than the Cubs love the Cubs. You can't manufacture that.

There were countless times where we would watch him walk. Our plane would go to the terminal, but the players don't go into the terminal—we would go down a special flight of stairs to go right to the bus. That set of stairs is usually a very rickety, wire/metal staircase. To watch Ron go up and down those stairs with those two artificial legs—it was hard to walk up and down those stairs with two regular legs—and no matter what, despite how late at night we would land, or coming home from spring training on the coldest day of the year, or returning from the longest road trip, you would see Ron Santo...and it would make it that much easier for you to get through the rest of your day.

The biggest thing we had to fear when Ron was doing a broadcast...was Ron. You never were really afraid, it was just Ron. You can't duplicate his realism because it was so original. He is an original character. There will be no one, ever, like him again. He loved the Cubs more than the Cubs love the Cubs. You can't manufacture that. It was weird. Ron's emotions rolled with the game unlike anybody else associated with the team. I've been with the team since 1998. When I first arrived on the scene with the Cubs, Ron was a constant. I watched different managers come in, making tons of money—I watched players come in who were All-Stars, but no one had that closeness and attachment to the team. Ron cared on a level that you could not manufacture.

You would see Ron and watch him walk. If you didn't know about the artificial legs, you wouldn't know. You could see that he didn't have a big stride, but you wouldn't know he was walking on prosthetic legs. Also, if you ever put your hands on his shoulders, it was the most amazing thing in the world. I've never felt another person's upper body that was that strong.

Without Ron, it has been tough. First of all, it's been a lot more expensive for me. I loved Ronnie for a thousand things, but the #1 thing I'll miss is that I will actually have spent all that money on my expense report. If Ron was within 15 feet of you...you couldn't buy a meal. You couldn't buy a drink. Ron was the host! I'll miss everything about him, and I'll definitely miss his wallet. The games were special just because Ron cared so much that it made you care more about the game that day. There are 162 games every year so it's hard to be fired up for every game. But, for Ron, every game was such a big deal that it would make you think of it as a big deal. I miss Ron's intensity more than anything.

TECH KNOW

MATT BOLTZ

Boltz has been WGN Cubs radio producer since 2001. He worked with Ron Santo and Pat Hughes on over 1,500 Cubs games, and he is currently in his eleventh year with WGN. Matt and Ron also spent considerable time together away from the ballpark, both before and, especially, after games.

I first started working with Ron during the 2001 season. For a kid that was 24 years old and starting out in radio with WGN with Pat Hughes and **RON SANTO***, I was starstruck. I tried to keep it together. The first time I walked into a booth at a spring training game in Mesa, both Ron and Pat walked in. It was the first time I had ever met them. I had talked to Pat on the phone once. Ron Santo said to me, "Kid, I've heard some good things about you. I understand that you've never done baseball. You stick with me, kid, and you're going to be just fine." Whether good or bad, I stuck with Ronnie. We had nothing but a great working relationship that turned into a very special friendship.

The first time my dad met Ron was in St. Louis. I have never seen my dad starstruck or short of words—ever. That was one of the first times that it hit me like, "Oh, my gosh! I'm working with a man that is not only a legend but that my own father is speechless around." It really touched me—here I was working

***SANTO**, in 1959, signed with the Cubs for $20,000, even though the Indians had offered him $50,000 and the Cincinnati Reds were the highest bidder with $80,000.*

with this man at WGN, who my dad had watched play for the Cubs—this was really something special.

For our WGN Cubs radio broadcasts, we use these Sennheiser headsets that have the microphone on them. Ron used to call them "earmuffs"—the headphones. Ron was so passionate, that if something would happen during the ballgame, he wouldn't think anything about taking these three or four hundred dollar headsets and just slamming them right on the counter. I can't tell you how many we went through my first year. I was sheepish. I didn't know what to do. I'm not going to tell Ron, "Hey, be careful. These are expensive." So, I'd go to my boss Jim Carollo and say, "We need to replace these." He'd send me out a couple, just in case, and say, "You've got to think of it this way, Matt. Ron's a ballplayer. This is just a piece of equipment. His headset is like his glove. When he gets upset, he's going to throw it down. There's nothing we can do about it. Just let him do his thing and try to stay out of his way."

> Ron's a ballplayer...His headset is like his glove. When he gets upset, he's going to throw it down.

The Cubs, in the way that they do, they blew a lead and lost a heartbreaking game. Here's Ronnie, just fuming, he picks up his headset, throws it and it took a second for me to realize that the headset had bounced into a cup of water. Now, we've got a live microphone going into a cup of water which didn't seem very safe. But, he didn't think twice about it. He just picked it up, kind of dusted it off and put the headset back on like nothing had happened. That was the tricky part, too. It was hard at first for me to get used to Ron because he was very unpredictable. During the game, if something would happen, he'd throw the headset down, so I would always have to keep an eye on Ron during the game. There's nothing worse than listening to something on the radio and there's a big thud from the microphone hitting the counter. I would watch him out of the corner of my eye, and I would always have my hand at his mike level. I could turn his mike on and off in a flash.

◇◇◇

Ron's attitude was really what made him look and feel the way he did. If he was hurting, he didn't really want anyone to know. During the 2010 season, he struggled quite a bit. I could tell because, when you're with someone day after day, you can see how it's wearing on them. He did keep things a secret. He always sounded good. I'd look him in the eye and say, "How are you feeling today, Ron?" He'd say, "Oh, Big Boy, I feel great!" I believed him! He always carried such a good attitude—even when he was hurting. There were days that he would come in and say, "Look, I had a little episode last night. I had an insulin reaction and I'm a little down today." But, as soon as that broadcast would start, as soon as that first pitch was thrown, he just had fire in his eye—like normal. He turned it on!

Since Ron had been doing this for a long time, he didn't have too many slip-ups when it came to profanity. I got to the point where I felt I had mastered this. But, I say that with tongue in cheek because there would be times when I'd have my headphones off for a minute or two and, sure enough, he would throw the headset or grab his cell phone because it was ringing and just start talking with the microphone right there. Once or twice, I did catch an "F-bomb". I don't know what it is with the booth in Houston but he got hit with a foul ball there. Towards the last few years he really relied on that monitor in the booth because it's really hard to see because of the shadows and how far we were from the field. He'd be staring at the monitor and there's a foul ball and I yelled, "Ronnie, look out! Foul ball!" All of a sudden Ron gets hit with a foul ball on the shoulder and he yells, "J---- ------!" I'll never forget it. The ball comes up and it just whistled past me. There was nothing I could do and we're live—we're not on delay. Pat, being the consummate professional, goes right into the next pitch. They'd have a little chuckle but they'd never look back. Ron was pretty good about censoring himself, for the most part.

◇◇◇

Pat is the straight man—I hear people say that. But, Pat is so well prepared. Ron's nickname for Pat was "The Professor". Pat would prepare, and then prepare some more, and then prepare even more. Ron's style was, "Look. I'm going to show up at the ballpark. I'm going to talk to some of the ballplayers. I'm going to talk to some of the coaches and the other broadcasters. I'll look over some notes and let's go." Pat's style is in preparing for a game immediately after the last broadcast has ended. In other words, he's always preparing for the next broadcast. He's careful of his words and very deliberate and well versed. That's why Ronnie would call Pat "The Professor" on the air. Ronnie would even tease him on the air. He'd say "Pat, you looked like a geek before you met me. You were nothing. You had the Coke bottle glasses. You had those Cosby sweaters." The Cubs used to do a "'70's night". They would promote it—"'70's night is coming up in a couple of days. The Cubs invite you to come on out and wear your gear and your garb and all this kind of stuff." Just like clockwork, Ron would say, "Oh, Patrick. The good news is that you don't have to go out and buy any costumes because you haven't bought any new clothes since the '70s." It was great. Listening to those guys go back and forth teasing each other was priceless.

> ...nine times out of ten, the food would end up on him, on his scorecard, on his bag, on his face.

◇◇◇

Ronnie's routine was more or less to start the pre-game show. There was a little segment he had to do in the beginning, then he'd step out and grab a plate from the dining room and he'd bring it back into the booth. I can't even tell you but nine times out of ten, the food would end up on him, on his scorecard, on his bag, on his face.

He would get scrambled eggs on his face. He'd be doing the game and an inning would go by and that egg would still be there. Me, Pat and maybe it was Cory Provus at the time, we'd have a running bet to see how long that egg would remain on his face. Pat would say, "Ronald Eggside is at the game today." Ron would kind of pause, look over at Pat and say, "Eggside. What does that mean, Patrick?" Pat would say, "I don't know, Ronnie. These are just notes that we get handed to us. I don't know who these people are." Ron would say, "I know it has something to do with eggs. I had eggs for breakfast." Then, Ron would figure it out and say, "Oh, I got eggs on my face!" It was just classic. We used to have a fictitious family. After Ron would knock something over, Pat would read a note from "the Spillers". The "Spillers" were great Cubs fans. They would always send notes to the booth. "The Spillers are here from Downers Grove." At first, Ronnie would go along. Then Pat would say, "It's the Spillers birthday today." Ron would say, "Oh, happy birthday to the Spillers." As the years went on Ron began to catch on. "Okay. You guys are making fun of me. I spilled something so the next half inning—the Spillers are here!" They had tons of stuff like that. A classic one was the "Spandexter" family. We were in Florida or **ATLANTA***. I guess Pat and Ron had gone to the gym this particular morning and Ron was riding a bike and some woman came in. She was a large woman, as the story goes—I wasn't there. This woman decided to do some stretches right there in front of Ron. She was wearing Spandex biker pants. Ron was so distracted by this large woman doing bends and stretches right in front of him, that he had to leave. Later in the day, we're all getting ready for the broadcast and Ron says, "Oh, this woman today—you should have seen it. It was terrible! I had to stop my workout. I couldn't concentrate." So, the next inning, Pat says, "Oh, the Spandexters are here

* *Baseball Prospectus* determined the precise Cubs game attended in the movie, "Ferris Bueller's Day Off." It was a 1985 game at Wrigley won by the **ATLANTA** Braves 4-2.

tonight! They arrived in a strrrrrretch limo." Ronnie laughed and spit his coffee projectile three seats in front of him. They had fun with food and clothes and hairpieces. You name it!

◇◇◇

Being around Ron and seeing people that met him for the first time—they were speechless. Like watching my father that first time. I compared the "Pat and Ron Show" to traveling with the Beatles. These guys had such a fan base. I didn't really grasp it until some of these moments. There'd be people standing in hotel lobbies waiting to get a glimpse of Pat and Ron. It was unbelievable.

◇◇◇

There was a time we were at the ballpark in **PHILADELPHIA***. Ron had had his surgeries. He would work out an arrangement with the clubhouse that they'd have a cab for him after the game. A lot of times we would join him so we didn't have to wait for the bus. There'd be a clubhouse attendant who would drive him around the ballpark, through the tunnels on the inside and out to meet a cab. On this day, when we showed up for the cab, some of the players had taken it. Ronnie was upset. He said, "Damn it! I need a cab. I'm not waiting for the bus!" The guy said, "We'll get to the other side of the ballpark and we'll find you one." So here are me, Ron Santo, and Cory Provus on this little golf cart, going on the sidewalk, the clubhouse guy is honking at people, people are pointing at Ron and he's waving like he's in a parade. It was hilarious. Of course, there were no cabs waiting on the other side. We did at least two—maybe three—laps around the ballpark. Occasionally, we had to stop for people and he'd sign an autograph.

---

*P. K. Wrigley and Milton Hershey were bitter business rivals.
When Wrigley bought the Chicago Cubs, Hershey tried to buy the
PHILADELPHIA Phillies…and sell chocolate gum. Hershey failed in
both efforts.

I spent ten years with Ron and he was so generous. He gave so much and he cared so much. He was a real guy and he was approachable. He wasn't standoffish. Overall, you could not meet a more generous and genuine human being. I think that's what set him apart. There was nothing phony about Ron—outside of his hairpiece. He really was authentic and a man of his word. An agreement with a handshake was all you needed from Ron. You didn't need a contract. He'd give you his word and he meant it.

◇◇◇

My second year we were up in Montreal. That started to become a burdensome trip for him just because of going through customs. The Cubs were leading early but ended up getting spanked. It was a long trip getting to the airport so it was a late night. Ronnie was wearing blue jeans. Don Baylor was a stickler on dress code. He wanted everyone wearing slacks and sports jackets. We're sitting on this tram to take us to the terminal. Baylor comes up to him and reminds Ron that jeans are not allowed on the charter. Ron looks at him, serious as can be and says, "These aren't blue jeans. These are Wranglers!" He said that all the time.

We get to the airport and there was a mechanical problem with the plane. Because we had to go through customs, we all had to carry our own bags. There were no airport people there to lug it for us. Because of Ron's leg issue, we had to pick up his bags, briefcase and stuff. They finally said the plane wasn't going to happen that night so we were going to have to stay at a Motel 6 across the street. By now it was 2:00 a.m. in Montreal. They told us that we'd have to grab our bags and walk across. We've got Sammy Sosa, **MOISES ALOU***, Todd Hundley, Pat, Chip Caray, Dave Otto, Joe Carter, some of the broadcasters—everyone. We're all grabbing our bags. Ron has his amputated leg so

*With the Expos in 1993, **MOISES ALOU** hit six consecutive home runs over a span of four games.

there's no way that he can walk a half mile across the street to get to this hotel. Chip Caray improvises and says, "Ronnie, let's see if we can get you a wheelchair." There was no one around and we couldn't find a wheelchair, anywhere. The only thing that we can find is a dolly that carries packages. He's saying, "Oh, my God. I'm not getting on that thing." We're asking, "Ronnie, what do you want to do?" They finally convince him to get on. Pat grabs his luggage. I've got his briefcase. Andy Masur has—I don't know—his toupee. Here's Ronnie, hanging on to this dolly with white knuckles. Chip Caray is pushing him through. There are potholes everywhere and Ronnie's yelling, "Oh, you meant to hit that! Damn it!" We're just laughing our butts off. Here is Cubs Legend Ron Santo being carted like a piece of luggage. It's one of my funniest memories.

I played golf with Ron in a tournament. He used to tease the hell out of me. I'm terrible. The only way I'll play is if there's free **BEER*** involved. Ron would have his golf tournaments. I didn't always have a chance to go. But, there was usually a good foursome of us that would go. I don't have golf clubs, so I borrowed a bag from my buddy. I kid you not. I broke two club heads on the tee. Ron is standing there. He says, "I like to watch each group go off and give you some advice." I've had a few beers and I know I'm terrible. So, I swing the club, the ball dribbles off the tee and the head goes flying. Ron screams, "J---- ------!" He's just laying into me and there's a big crowd. He says, "There is nothing I can tell you that will help you. The best advice I have for you is to sit on the cart and just keep drinking." So I did.

He even ripped me the next day on the air.

He was so gullible, too. You'd be telling a story and he'd say, "Oh, is that right, Big Boy?"

*In 1984, Santo did an ad for the Miller Brewing Company that was to run in the 1984 World Series—if the Cubs would have made the World Series.

He was so funny. We all know how passionate he was about the game. We joked that Andy Masur was his caddy. On the road, Ron would need help. When Andy left to go to work for the Padres, he said to me, "Hey, Big Boy. I'd really like you to help me out." I started helping him and really saw a side of Ronnie that humbled me—watching him get ready for bed; taking his legs off; needing help just setting up his room at night. There were a lot of things we had to go through each night on the road such as making sure that he was near an outlet where the phone would work. I got a call one night. I'm in Milwaukee. In the middle of the night, the phone rings and I hear, "Boltzy!" I say, "Ron, are you okay? I'm comin' over." He says, "Okay." I'm freaking out. In this case, we had adjoining rooms. Whenever we could, we'd have rooms that were next to each other. We always left a crack open so that we could get in and out. I run in there and say, "Ron, what's wrong?" He says, "Umm. I can't find the remote control and it's stuck on this infomercial and I can't stand watching this anymore." Here he his calling me in the middle of the night and I think it's an emergency. He needs me to change the channel because he can't find the remote! Usually when he couldn't find it, it was under his arm or under the pillow that was tucked in next to him. He'd say, "Oh, Big Boy. I'm so sorry." I'd help him to his room at night. Our routine was, we'd go to the bar and have a couple of cocktails. I'd help him up to his room

> "I want you to know, Big Boy, that if I die that you'll just be a footnote in the article. Okay?"

and get him settled in and say, "Okay, Ronnie. I'm going to go back down. I'm in the hotel. I'm meetin' some of the other guys. If you need anything, call my cell phone." He'd yell, "You know what? You don't care. You're going to go out and drink. I'm gonna be up here. I could have a heart attack, but that's fine. I'll die and no one will ever care. But, I want you to know, Big Boy, that if I die that you'll just be a footnote in the article. Okay?" I'd say, "Thanks a lot, Ronnie." I'd joke back, "As long as you're on my watch, you're not going to pass away. When you get home, that's your family's problem. Don't worry. I've got your back." He'd say, "Oh, I love ya, pal." He told me on many occasions that I felt like a son to him and he felt like a father figure to me. It meant a lot to me at his funeral when the family asked me to help and be a part of the pall bearers that got him in there. His son Jeff and I have gotten pretty close over the years. Jeff is a great guy. He called me the night that Ron passed but before they decided to remove the respirator. He said, "We know that Ron would have wanted you to know before. You're part of the family." To be that close to a man that had such a big impact... I know that there is no one else in my life that I'll ever know that's so popular, that was such a giving, bigger-than-life person. He always gave 110% to this world. He was such a great soul. When I hung up the phone after Jeff called, I was lost for words. In fact, when Jeff called me, he didn't even say it. I could hear it in his voice and just said, "Oh, no." He said, "Yes." He said, "Could you please call Judd Sirott and Andy Masur and Cory Provus and let those guys know. I know that my dad would want them to know." I just sat there. I felt empty. I felt sick but, honestly, it didn't kick in right away. It was December and I usually don't see Ron until the Cubs Convention. I got a hold of all of them on the first try and they were stunned. They wanted to know what happened. Jeff had explained some, but nobody knew a lot. Just talking to those guys choked me up because I couldn't believe we were actually talking about this. We all knew that one day it could happen, but when it hits you in the face like that—everyone was just stunned.

Ronnie had such a huge impact on me. And, Pat and Ron—both of those guys—just watching them together—there'll never be anything like it.

Pat is awesome. Right when I got the job—when I was hired in February 2001, I was still working at a station in Columbia, Missouri and wrapping things up with that job. I came home and on my answering machine was, "Hi, Matt Boltz. It's Pat

Hughes calling. It's February 21 at 8:00 p.m. and I just want you to know that I look forward to working with you. We're going to have some fun. You be yourself, enjoy yourself. If you ever need anything from me, just let me know." When I finally met them out in Mesa, Pat and Ron both put their arms around me and made me feel so welcome. To this day, I still consider Pat a close friend. It's my family—sometime it's dysfunctional. They made me feel part of the broadcast and part of the Cubs radio family that we have.

The last phone conversation I had with Ron, I was flying out— we were doing a game for **NORTHWESTERN*** down in Texas. We're on the plane and we're taxiing. Here's Ron calling on my cell phone. I thought that I'd pick it up real quick and tell him that I'd call him tomorrow. He says, "Hey, Big Boy!" I said, "Ronnie, how're you doin'?" He says, "I'm doin' good. I had this little procedure—waiting to hear back but I feel good. I can't wait to see you at the Cubs Convention. We'll get together up in my room and have some drinks. Can't wait. Now, where are you?" I say, "I'm on a plane with Northwestern." He says, "Oh, college." I say, "Yeah." Ron says, "I gotta question. Do they serve booze on that plane?" I tell him, "Ronnie, it's college kids. It's against the rules." He say, "Oh, okay. Did anyone bring any booze with them?" I say, "Well no, Ronnie. It's college kids. You can't do that." He says, "Oh, okay. What kind of plane is it?" I'm like,

*<u>**NORTHWESTERN**</u> is the only member school of an NCAA major conference that has never made it to the NCAA basketball tournament; however, in 1939 and 1956, Northwestern hosted the Final Four.... Lou Saban, the Northwestern football coach in 1955, hired George Steinbrenner as his assistant coach. Steinbrenner was a graduate assistant under Woody Hayes at Ohio State and also a football assistant at Purdue.... In 1972, Steinbrenner tried to buy the Cleveland Indians. When he was rebuffed, he put together a syndicate to buy the Yankees....Steinbrenner was an original part-owner of the Chicago Bulls....The New York Yankees are the most valuable major league baseball franchise with a worth of 1.5 billion dollars. It is located in the poorest congressional district in the United States.

"Ron, we're going down the runway." He says, "Well, what kind of plane is it?" I tell him, "It's one of these little jets." He say, "Is it a jet or a prop?" I say, "It's a jet—but a small one." He says, "Oh, there's no way I'd get on that thing. Those things are not safe at all! Those things go down all the time." I say, "Hey, Ronnie. Thanks for that." He's just crackin' up. He says, "Oh, Big Boy, you know I'm playin' with ya. I love ya. Give me a call in a few days and have a safe trip." He's asking me about booze, teasing me about going down in a plane—as I'm taking off—just what I'd expect. That was the last time I talked to him.

> Knowing Ronnie, though, he probably would have wanted to expire in the booth.

I was one of the pallbearers at Ronnie's funeral. Right before we received the casket from some of his ex-teammates, I said to Judd Sirott, "How many nights did we take Ronnie up to his room? How many nights did we stumble him back to his room after a long night of boozin' it up on the road? You know what? Let's take him to his room one more time." That's just how we felt. It was fitting. It was a chance for me to say goodbye, even though I wish I would have had a better chance to speak to him. At the same time, knowing Ron, that's the way he would have wanted it. The way it happened, he was at home. He was with his family. It wasn't on the road. It wasn't in the booth. I'm happy that it did happen that way so that he could be with his family. Knowing Ronnie, though, he probably would have wanted to expire in the booth.

TAKE THIS JOB AND LOVE IT

ANDY MASUR

Masur is a Chicago native and lifelong Cubs fan who spent eight years at WGN working with "Pat & Ron" beginning in 1999. The Bradley grad is currently in his fifth season as a radio play-by-play man for the San Diego Padres.

I started working with Ron in '99 and left right after the '06 season—eight full seasons. Growing up, I listened to Ronnie a lot. Also, he played in the first game I ever saw at Wrigley Field. For my fifth birthday, my parents took me to a Cubs-Giants game in May, 1972. He was in the lineup playing third base. My dad knew him more as a player while I, of course, heard him as a broadcaster. I was well versed in Cubs history growing up in Glenview as a third-generation Cub fan. Ron Santo actually lived in Glenview for a while....

FRANK SINATRA*, Jr. was singing during the seventh inning stretch one game. Our booth was so small that I had to give up my seat for the person who came in to be interviewed before singing. Frank Sinatra, Jr. was convinced that Santo was a pitcher. He kept going on and on, "I saw you pitch. You were great." Ron, being Ron, just sat there saying, "Yeah. Yeah. Yeah." Santo knew his father and they had dinner with him a few

---

*Bobby Thomson hit "The Shot Heard Around the World" on October 3, 1951... **FRANK SINATRA** and Jackie Gleason were at the game. When Thomson homered off Ralph Branca, Dodger fan Gleason did a technicolor yawn (vomited) on Sinatra's shoes...In the movie *The Godfather*, Sonny Corleone died while listening to that game... Dave Winfield was born that day.

times in Palm Springs. Ron didn't want to embarrass Jr., but he never pitched for the Cubs.

I was with him at his house in the spring of 2003 when he found out he didn't get into the Hall of Fame. I was sitting on the couch right next to him when the phone rang, and it wasn't the Hall. Just to see the dejected look on his face.... I don't think I'd ever seen him so down about something, but he tried to keep that brave face because there was a lot of media and cameras in the room with him at the same time. I know that in '03 he really felt strongly that was going to be the year he would get in. Looking at his face, you didn't know whether to hug him or pat him on the back and say, "Hey, it's okay," or "I'm really sorry." It meant a lot to him at that point.

Fast forward about six months from that day—the Cubs told him they were going to retire his jersey at the end of the year. The day he found out about that, it was like his birthday. There was such joy on his face. He was making phone calls left and right, calling his wife, his kids, his friends. They had a press conference, and I was standing outside the door of the press conference room and was going on the radio with it. He knew I was on the air live. He comes up to me, gives me a huge hug, goes, "All right. This is great, Big Boy!" Then he goes into the room and answers all the questions.

The one thing that I really noticed about Ron was his relationship with the team and players. Every player that was in that clubhouse for even a couple of days knew who Ron was. Ron made a point to go up and talk to them and say hello. They respected the hell out of that guy. They might make fun of him because of something he may have said on the air, but, deep down, that team and those guys in that clubhouse always had a great respect for him not only for what he did on the field but what he was doing off-the-field dealing with all the things he was going through healthwise, and still finding time to go out and raise money for JDRF. He wasn't with us during the 2003 playoffs because that was when he found out he had bladder cancer.

Kerry Wood, who was probably Ron's closest friend on the team, seemed to look up to Ron maybe not like a father but more like a grandfather because of the age difference. Kerry made sure that Ron's jersey #10 was hanging in the dugout for each of the playoff games. When they beat the Braves in Atlanta, everybody was in the main clubhouse celebrating and throwing champagne around, Kerry Wood and a couple of other players went into another hallway, picked up their phone, called Ron and were pouring champagne on each other while Ron was listening on the phone. That meant so much to him that I can't even say. I'm starting to tear up just talking about it. It seemed so cruel and so unfair.

◇◇◇

Ron always wanted to do the pre-game interview with the players on the road. So, I would go with him and would hold the recorder because I can't tell you how many times he'd go down there by himself and we'd come back up to the booth, and the interview wouldn't be there because he forgot to hit the record button or he thought he was hitting the record button and he'd hit the stop button instead. I decided after a couple of those episodes that I was going to go down with him. The conversations that would go on before the interview with the manager were priceless—I wish we could air those because they were hilarious. Ron would be questioning things, saying, "I'm not second-guessing. I just want to know." He'd go through this whole thing. Names were awful for him. For as long as we knew each other, I would often be called "Big Boy". If he forgot your name, it would be "Big Boy." That was the way he got around it.

A pitcher came to us in 1999 on a trade, Ruben Quevedo, who the Cubs eventually traded to Milwaukee. There was a night game in '01 against the Brewers. Pat goes through the starting lineups, who's pitching for the Cubs—who's pitching for the

Brewers. The pitcher for the Brewers was Ruben Quevedo, who we had on our team before. Ron is stunned.

We get on the air, and he says, "You know, Pat, this guy out there on the mound reminds me of somebody. He looks familiar." Pat, and all of us, never want to throw him under the bus on the air because we all respected him too much. We get to the break. We tell Ron that Quevedo was with us. "No, no, it's somebody else. I'm telling you. It's somebody else." I'm sitting up on the second row in the booth running through the Internet thinking, "Who could he possibly think this is? There's nobody else who fits the criteria, who used to pitch for us recently and is now pitching for the Brewers. It could only be Quevedo." We get to the third inning. Ron is hell-bent that this is somebody else. But then it hits him. All of a sudden...Pat is in the middle of a call...you hear Ron start to giggle. Pat, in his infinite way, goes, "Ron, did something strike you as funny in that call?" "No, Pat, I've got to tell you something right now. It WAS Quevedo." He'd gone for three innings convincing himself and convincing us that it was somebody else, and finally he realized it was the same guy.

◇◇◇

In getting to know Ron, with all the little bumps in the road that he had, he always came through it...he always persevered...he always had this disposition and this outlook that he was going to get by it. He was going to get past it, and the only thing that mattered to him was spring training. Most of these things that he had done were in the off-season, so he was always looking toward spring training.

I saw Ron for the last time in August of 2010 at Wrigley Field at the Padres-Cubs game. I had a nice moment to catch up with Ron in the booth before he left. He gave me a huge bear hug— which he always did! He goes, "I'm so proud of you, Big Boy! I miss you, but I'm so proud of you." I told him, "You know, Ron, we'll see you in San Diego when you guys come out toward the end of the year. It'll be great to see you. We'll go out and have a good time. Be well." He goes, "All right, pal." He left the booth, and that was the last conversation I had with him. He didn't make the trip to San Diego because he was not feeling well.

Then I got a phone call from Matt Boltz the Thursday night just before he passed. You get these inklings that, when a person you are friends with but don't talk to on the phone a lot, all of a sudden calls you...and you know what the phone call is about. That's what it was. I was so shaken that night.

The first thing I did was to go back to all the hard drives and flash drives I had with all the audio of myself and Matt and Pat and Ron. I sat at my computer for about four hours. I put together an 18-20 minute montage of some of the greatest moments that we'd had in the booth together. I sent copies to Pat and Matt with an e-mail that said, "Listen, this is a tough day, and I know it was a tough night for all of us. We need to remember Ronnie like he'd want us to. We need to smile! We need to laugh!"

> ...when a person you are friends with but don't talk to on the phone a lot... calls you...and you know what the phone call is about.

Again, I didn't sleep that night because I knew my phone was going to be ringing with calls from people who knew I was very close to him. Sure enough, being on the West Coast when those Midwest morning shows are going on at five o'clock when it's three in the morning here, my phone begins to ring. I was a basket case that Friday.

When I had gotten it all together and was able to leave my apartment for the first time that Friday night, after trying to get hold of Pat Hughes the whole day, Pat called me back. I was standing outside of a bar in downtown San Diego because a buddy of mine was celebrating a birthday. I excused myself and walked outside and Pat got me going again. Pat said, "You think you were gone from the booth...you were never gone. Ronnie asked about you all the time. He loved you, Andy."... and, I lost it! Right there, on the street. It's indescribable.

The Padres play the Cubs early in the year—in April. Our booths are next to each other, separated only by a glass window. And, I'm not going to see Ron there. It's still not closed for me because of that whole thing that is lingering there for me in the future.

This is how a ton of people felt about him. Ron made everybody feel like they were the most important thing to him at that time. I'll never forget the first time my dad met him. He made my dad light up. It's not often that a son gets to see his dad in awe. My dad's thinking, "Oh my God. You're working with Ron Santo. I watched this guy play! I know who this is, but I've never met him. Now, I know him." Ron would always ask about my folks, my brothers, my nieces no matter what was going on with him.

The thing Ron was most concerned about was my love life. Or lack thereof. He was a prince. I've thought about him every day since I got back from the funeral. I flew to Chicago for the funeral. Listening to everybody tell all the stories, it all just came back.

It's amazing what an impact Ron had.

WE'LL BE BACK RIGHT AFTER THIS

CORY PROVUS

Chicago native, Cory Provus, worked with "Pat & Ron" on WGN Cubs radio broadcasts for two seasons, 2007 and 2008. The Syracuse grad is now in his third year in Milwaukee working with Bob Uecker on Brewers radio.

My wife, Dana, who was then my fiancé, came out to Arizona for spring training. We had a free night so Dana and I had dinner with Ron and Vicki Santo. This was a couple of weeks after Ron turned 70.

The four of us are chit-chatting and about an hour into the dinner, I said, "So, how is 70? Have you had any senior moments since turning 70?" After about two seconds, Ron goes, "Nah, everything is fine." Then all of a sudden, I hear this loud bang on the table. It was Vicki's hand. She said, "Excuse me?" Ronnie was like, "What? What's wrong?" She said, "Don't you want to tell them about what happened the other day with the television?" I was thinking to myself, "Oh, this is going to be good."

Ronnie said, "Oh, okay. I guess there was one thing." Ronnie was sitting on the sofa in his house in Scottsdale watching TV. He wanted to change the channel from 5 to 12. He kept hitting 1-2, 1-2, 1-2...but it wasn't changing. He got new batteries and replaced the old ones. He hit 1-2, 1-2, 1-2...but the TV was not changing channels. He's getting frustrated and really getting upset. He yelled, "Vicki, I need you." Vicki answered, "All right, hang on one second." He said, "No. I need you now. I can't change the TV channel. I'm really trying to change the channel. I want to watch something else." Vicki comes in and says, "Okay, what's wrong?" Ronnie says, "Vicki, look. I have the remote in my hand. I'm hitting 1-2, 1-2, and it's not changing channels." Vicki says, "Ron, do you want to know why that's not changing channels?" Ron yells out, "WHY?" She said, "Because that's not the remote. That's your cell phone!" When I heard that, I just fell off my chair. I could just imagine Ronnie trying to change the channel and is hitting 1-2 on his cell phone repeatedly!

◇◇◇

I'm 32 years old. Pat's first year with the Cubs was '96, the year I graduated high school. I grew up listening to the Cubs, listening to Harry Caray and Pat Hughes, and I knew Ron Santo's name from day one. I'm a third-generation Cub fan. I remember hearing my dad's stories about Ron Santo as a player. Then, as I got older, Pat and Ron became part of my summer. It was amazing that here I was working with these guys for two years and traveling with them and calling them dear friends.

My dad was amazed that I was working with them. He's the kind of guy who wanted autographs. After each season, he always wants a ball from the people I work with in the booth. After my first year, I got a ball, signed my name on it, got Ron's name on it, Pat's name, and Matt Boltz. We did that two years in Chicago, and I've done it now two years in **MILWAUKEE***, as well, working with Bob Uecker. It wasn't just my dad. It's very rare when a parent can see a child truly living their dream. My parents are divorced and both remarried, but to see all four of my parents be able to come into the booth and see their son living their dream—being a big-league announcer, it's an emotional moment, I know, for them...and for me.

---

*The **MILWAUKEE** Braves (1953-1965) are the only MLB franchise that never had a losing season.

We were at Wrigley Field, and it was '70's night.' The guest sing-ing *Take Me Out to the Ball Game* was Barry Williams, who played Greg Brady on *The Brady Bunch*. The person singing the stretch would always come into the booth and interview with Pat and Ron in the bottom of the sixth inning. I was doing the interview that day. Barry Williams was in our booth, and we're referencing *The Brady Bunch* a lot. Ron must have called him "Greg" 30 times during the interview—over and over again. Barry Williams was great about it. He was not going to show up Ron Santo.

In talking about it later, Ron laughed at himself and said, "Oh, I'm sure I did that. That's okay." Ronnie was fine just being able to laugh at himself about it. That's one reason it was always a treat to get to work with the guy. He was always fun to be around. Part of my job at the ballpark was to make sure the interview got recorded. He would tape the *Lou Piniella Show,* but it was my job to record it. So it would be Ron, Lou and me in Lou's office every day taping an interview, which would be five minutes long.

But those two guys would be at it for half an hour. I would sit there—here I was 28-29 years old listening to two baseball leg-ends talk about the game, talk about their playing days. If you're trying to learn the game, and learn its history, you couldn't ask for a better seminar than that. Listening to these two guys—Lou would be talking about **BILLY MARTIN*** and Steinbrenner, and Santo was talking about Leo Durocher. They talked about the sixties and guys they played with. It was fasci-nating to just sit there. I would rarely say a word unless they

---

*In 1974 **BILLY MARTIN** was managing the Texas Rangers and Frank Lucchesi was his third base coach. Martin tried using a transistor hook-up to his coaches to relay signals. One game the system was broken, but Martin kept yelling instructions for a suicide squeeze into the microphone. Red Sox pitcher Luis Tiant finally stepped off the mound and yelled: "Frank, Billy said he wanted the suicide squeeze."

asked me something. Lou was tremendous. That was my favorite part of my job—listening to Ron and Lou share those memorable stories.

My first Cubs broadcast was spring training 2007, the last exhibition game before the season began. We were in Las Vegas playing Seattle on Saturday, and we were to open in Cincinnati on Monday. I was nervous as all heck. I had just gotten the job five days before. I was in **BIRMINGHAM***, Alabama on a Monday, the day I got the job. I had to leave Alabama Wednesday, go to Chicago, unpack, repack, get on a plane...and I was on the air with Pat and Ron that Saturday in Vegas! It was a crazy week.

I was really nervous. I don't think I had a very good broadcast. I'm on the Cubs charter for the first time, going to Cincinnati. I'm sitting against the window, with an empty seat to my right. I'm not saying much because I don't know what I'm supposed to be doing. I'm not too happy because I think I had a bad broadcast. About halfway through the flight, Ron Santo comes back and sits with me. He must have sat there for an hour. He talked to me, told me to just be myself, have some fun, relax. "You have tremendous talent. You're going to be a great addition to our booth." For him to sit there with me for an hour, saying all these encouraging things to me meant the world to me at that time. I couldn't believe that Ron Santo would do that for me. I'll never forget that. I feel it's a big reason why I'm in the position I'm in today.

I talked to Ron on Monday of the week he died. My wedding was just a few weeks away and Ronnie and Vicki were invited to my wedding. They could not come, but we talked every couple of weeks. This particular time, he called and always wanted to know what was going on with the Brewers. He also wanted to know where I was registered. We were able to mix in baseball

---

*The New England Patriots once played a regular-season home game in **BIRMINGHAM**, Alabama, in September 1968.

with talking about serving ware from Crate and Barrel. It was a vintage Cory-Ron conversation where we covered a bit of everything. I remember thinking he didn't sound great during that call. I talked to my wife as soon as I hung up the phone and said to her, "Ron did not sound good."

Then, Matt Boltz called me Thursday night around 9:30 p.m. and told me what was going on with Ron. I didn't sleep at all that night. I finally got out of bed around 3:00 a.m. and saw the notice of his death when it hit the wires. I spent all morning listening to the coverage on WGN-TV and WGN Radio. It was a real, real tough day for me...like it was for millions.

When Ron died, there were a couple of things that came to mind. There was the funny part—the funny moments when we'd joke around. We always had a saying when Ron and I would do this pre-game bit. We do about a five-minute cross talk, and it was great. As soon as we'd go to break, Ron would put his headset down and leave the booth. Matt Boltz and I, after doing the five-minute bit, would act like Ron was done for the day because he was leaving the booth. We'd say, "Santo. Great job today. We'll see you in Houston." We must have said 'Houston' for three months. Finally, one day after we said it to him, he stopped...did not open the door. He said, "Let me ask you something. Why is it always Houston? You've been saying Houston for three months. Why can't you say 'see you in Pittsburgh' or '**CINCINNATI**'*? Why is it always Houston?"

One Cub Central pre-game at Wrigley Field, Ron and I were talking about the game. Carlos Zambrano was starting that

*In April of 1957, Don Hoak of the **REDS** was on second base and Gus Bell was on first when Wally Post hit a double-play ground ball. Hoak fielded the ball with his bare hands and tossed the ball to Johnny Logan, the Milwaukee Braves shortstop. Hoak was automatically out for interference—but not the batter—and the Reds thereby avoided an easy double-play. The Reds did the same subterfuge three times that year before the rule was changed.

particular day. His previous start he had to leave about the sixth inning because of what we thought at the time was cramps in his right forearm. We later found out that he actually had a low potassium count.

Ron and I are live on the network and talking about it. I said, "Ron, you know Carlos Zambrano is back out there today, six days removed from having had to leave because of what we thought was cramping in his forearm. We have since learned that his potassium was low. In talking with him, we've learned he has upped his fluids all week long, and his potassium is good. Sure enough, he ate plenty of bananas to get himself ready." Ronnie heard that and he goes, "Yeah, bananas are good, but if you eat too many, it'll plug you up." I am dying! I'm dying and we still had a long way to go. I still had to read sponsor things. After about five seconds, I can't compose myself. I'm dying on the air laughing. I finally try to get the ship going and say to Ron, "That's right. Good point, Ron." But, to try to bring him back into the conversation—he's gone. He realizes what he said. He takes his headset off. You can hear the mike hitting the table. I had to continue. I cannot stop laughing. I'm trying to read these promos, these sponsor charts, and tease what's coming up in the pre-game. For the life of me, I'm having the hardest time doing it because Ron Santo just said—on the air—that eating too many bananas would plug you up. That is one of my favorite Ron Santo Cub Special pre-game stories.

◇◇◇

When he came to Milwaukee the last two years, we'd always pick a night to meet at the Pfister Hotel and have a drink and catch up and laugh and reminisce about stories. He'd always want to know about my wife. Ron had a big influence on who I married.

When I got the Cub job, I was 28 years old, single and was back in my home town of Chicago. I was having a great time dating. Ronnie would always ask me what was going on—who I was dating. I'd tell him that I was going out a lot...but he didn't believe me. He wanted to meet these girls. After a couple of dates, I'd bring the girl up to the booth during a game for her to meet Pat and Ron and Matt. Ronnie would be like, "Okay. That one's okay."

Sometime in August, 2008, I brought up a girl named Dana. She was probably the fifth girl I had brought up to the booth. I introduced her to the guys. No big deal. She leaves to go back down to her seat. We're not back from our break yet, and Ronnie turns to me and says, "Provus, that's by far the best one you've brought up here. That one's a keeper!" Well...that's the girl I ended up marrying.

Ron loved country music, and he loved Toby Keith. His cell phone ring was often a Toby Keith song, *"I Want to Talk About Me, I Want to Talk About I, I Want to Talk About #1."* He tried to remember to either give me his phone or to turn it off when he taped the Lou Piniella show. I can't tell you how many times we were taping the manager of the Cubs doing our pre-game interview, and sure enough—we hear Toby Keith in the background, "I Want to Talk About Me..." You'd hear the microphone rattling around, as Ronnie tried to get the phone out of his pocket to quiet it. Lou sometimes would sing along with it. Sometimes he wouldn't even reference it. Sometimes he would listen to the lyrics and incorporate that into his interview.

The Ron Santo who was on the air was the Ron Santo who was next to you on the plane. It was the Ron Santo who would shake your hand before getting on the bus in Houston. Ron was exactly the same person he was on the air that he was off the air. That resonated with Cub fans because they felt the same pain he was going through, that he endured.

That played into the popularity of the Pat and Ron Show. I had a front-row seat and was part of the ride for a couple of years... some of the best moments of my life.

HEAR AND NOW

JUDD SIROTT

Sirott worked with "Pat & Ron" on Cubs WGN radio broadcasts in both 2009 and 2010. With an extensive background of hockey announcing, he currently serves as the Chicago Blackhawks studio/analyst on WGN radio. The Chicago native is in his third season working on Cubs radio.

Ron Santo was a guy who had a gigantic heart. One of the things that, over the last couple of years, he was really tuned into was his daughter Linda, who was battling cancer. We're talking about a man who was *the* most positive guy ever. He tried to infuse that into his daughter as she was trying to battle her way through cancer. There were times where it was difficult for him to do games because all he could think about was Linda. He worried about how she was doing because it was such a difficult process for her.

We were in Pittsburgh and Ronnie finally got a call from his daughter that she had a successful operation—that she would be fine. If everything went as hoped, and as expected, she would be able to comfortably rehabilitate and hopefully be cancer free. Ronnie became a changed man! It had been such a weight on him. I talked with Linda at the funeral, and she was doing really well. Linda said, "I know my dad had the chance to see me get better, and that means a lot to me."

◇◇◇

Ronnie got hit in the head by Jack Fisher in 1966. It shook him up quite a bit, and he talked about it a lot when guys would get knocked down or take a head shot. He would say how the time he had been hit had impacted him, and how difficult it is when you first come back to try and be the same hitter you were before. The Mets' David Wright always had a special place in Ronnie's heart not only because he was a third-baseman, but he loved the way Wright played the game—he loved his talent. Wright also got drilled in the head.

I'd never seen this before, but it was very difficult for Ronnie in visiting parks to make his way into the dugout. He would only do it on special occasions. We went to New York, a city Ronnie hated. Ronnie made a point of going into the dugout, and he asked the Mets PR man Jay Horwitz to please bring David Wright over because he wanted to have a conversation with David in the Cubs dugout. Think about that! Although Ronnie hated the Mets, his mind was really on David Wright and how he was doing. David came over and had that conversation with Ronnie. For David to have a guy of that stature have that kind of conversation with him left a lasting impression...but that was Ronnie!

◇◇◇

For the recorded pre-game interviews, Ronnie would always do questions about "where are we?" Ronnie would always have to record the manager. And on the road, he would also do the player interview. This would happen all the time—he would grab a guest, find a quiet spot somewhere in the clubhouse, and they would sit down. Ronnie would clear his throat, "Okay, all right, Ron Santo here to start game one of a three-game series against.... oh my God, where are we?" "Cincinnati, Ronnie." "Okay. Ron Santo back here in—oh my God, where are we?" "Cincinnati, Ronnie." But that would happen everywhere. He would always forget where we were.

One of Ronnie's favorite sayings was, "I'm not media...I'm a Cub." A lot of people chided him about his craft. "I'm not an announcer—I'm me!" We'd all just laugh when he would say that.

◇◇◇

Ron would be forgetful about a whole mess of stuff and would get facts wrong. He would mention some sort of a fact, "This guy had 30 home runs each of the last four years." And then, there would be dead silence from Pat. Ronnie would then just say, "Okay, if I'm wrong, just tell me I'm wrong. Don't be silent and say nothing. Just tell me I'm wrong. All right?"

People would come up to the booth constantly. It was great. I personally loved it. It was a parade into the booth to meet Pat and Ron and to get a chance to see that view of Wrigley Field, which is absolutely breathtaking, and to get a chance to shoot the breeze with Pat and Ron. People would come up, and Ronnie wouldn't even know who they were, not because he'd forget, he just didn't know who they were. I remember people would walk out and we would ask Ronnie, "Who was that?" "I have no clue."

One of my favorite things is a rain delay. Why? I have no idea... because it usually made for a long game. During rain delays, people at Wrigley Field would hang around. We'd all be in the booth. Ronnie would be either making phone calls or chit-chatting with people in the booth. Invariably, someone in the crowd would yell up to Ronnie, "Hey, Ron." Ronnie would stand up, lean down and yell, "What?" "Will you sign a ball?" "Yeah, throw one up here." Then they'd toss up a hat or a ball, and Ronnie would sign it and throw it back down. It was like a scene out of *The Honeymooners*. Ralph Kramden yelling out the window at Norton, or yelling at somebody on the street.

My predecessors and I were Pat and Ron's laugh track. They were so funny, and we had so much fun. One time in San Diego, we were in the booth and, due to its location, there can be a limited view of the field. A fan stood up, blocking their view. Pat said, "Right now, there is a gentleman who is standing up, and I cannot see home plate...I cannot see the umpire...I cannot see who's hitting, so Ronnie, why don't you take over?" For some reason, Ronnie thought that when he took his headset off, that was like the mute button, so people couldn't hear what

In Loving Memory

Ronald Edward Santo

February 25, 1940—December 3, 2010

"I'm like those fans out there. I'm a Cubs fan. All I care about is if the Cubs win."

IN LOVING MEMORY OF RONALD EDWARD SANTO
HOLY NAME CATHEDRAL
FRIDAY, DECEMBER 10, 2010
10:00 A.M.

CELEBRANT   MONSIGNOR DANIEL G. MAYALL, HOLY NAME CATHEDRAL

PALLBEARERS

ERNIE BANKS	FERGUSON JENKINS
GLENN BECKERT	RAY SCARPELLI
RANDY HUNDLEY	BILLY WILLIAMS

INTRODUCTORY RITES

GREETING, SPRINKLING OF HOLY WATER AND PLACING OF THE PALL

ENTRANCE PROCESSION—BE NOT AFRAID, BY ROBERT J. DUFFORD, S. J.

YOU SHALL CROSS THE BARREN DESERT,
BUT YOU SHALL NOT DIE OF THIRST.
YOU SHALL WANDER FAR IN SAFETY
THOUGH YOU DO NOT KNOW THE WAY.

YOU SHALL SPEAK YOUR WORDS IN FOREIGN LANDS
AND ALL WILL UNDERSTAND.
YOU SHALL SEE THE FACE OF GOD AND LIVE.

REFRAIN: BE NOT AFRAID.
I GO BEFORE YOU ALWAYS.
COME FOLLOW ME,
AND I SHALL GIVE YOU REST.

IF YOU PASS THROUGH RAGING WATERS
IN THE SEA, YOU SHALL NOT DROWN.
IF YOU WALK AMIDST THE BURNING FLAMES,
YOU SHALL NOT BE HARMED.

IF YOU STAND BEFORE THE POWER OF HELL
AND DEATH IS AT YOUR SIDE,
KNOW THAT I AM WITH YOU, THROUGH IT ALL.

REFRAIN

BLESSED ARE YOUR POOR,
FOR THE KINGDOM SHALL BE THEIRS.
BLEST ARE YOU THAT WEEP AND MOURN,
FOR ONE DAY YOU SHALL LAUGH.

AND IF WICKED MEN INSULT AND HATE YOU, ALL BECAUSE OF ME,
BLESSED, BLESSED ARE YOU!

REFRAIN

OPENING PRAYER

LITURGY OF THE WORD

Walkin' with Ernie Banks

The Sporting News

Vol. 168, No. 8   SEPTEMBER 6, 1969   Price: 50 Cents

RON SANTO
Cub Firebrand

With young daughter Linda

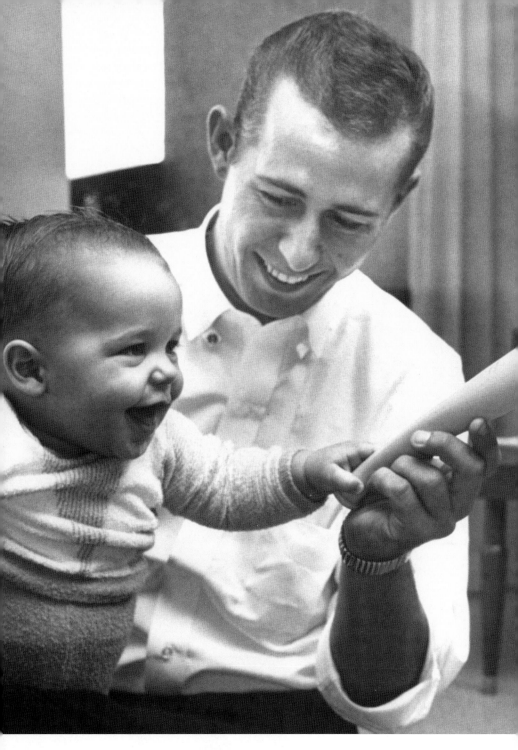

With son Ronnie Jr.

Interviewing with Tony Kubek (above) and Sandy Koufax (right)

Mr. Softball 1975—Glenview

Daughter Linda throwing out first pitch on March 10, 2011 at Hohokam Park in Mesa—"Ron Santo Day"

Posin' with Milton Berle and Leo Durocher

Santo and Glenn Beckert show off their Gold Gloves

Ron Santo and Michael Jordan—
Separated at birth

With a little help from Fergie Jenkins on the left

Enjoying the grandkids, Sam and Spencer

Pat Hughes, Ron Santo, Hank Aaron, Ernie Banks, Billy Williams

The Cubs infield celebrates Ron Santo Day
Don Kessinger, Glenn Beckert and Joe Pepitone

Dick Butkus back in the day

Celebrating son Jeff's wedding 10/10/10

Ron Santo and Glenn Beckert—Pizza Guys OK, maybe the sandwiches were expensive.

Sports Illustrated

JUNE 30, 1969   5

THE RAUCOUS NEW CUBS

Ron Santo leads off first

he said. He took off his headset, put it down, stands up...and starts screaming at this guy, "Will you please sit down! Will you please sit down! Will you please sit down, sir. Excuse me, will you please sit down." He just kept yelling at this guy, and Matt Boltz and I are absolutely crying. All you can hear is Ronnie screaming in the background. The guy wasn't that far away. I don't know if he was slow or if there was something wrong with him, but he wasn't getting the message.

◇◇◇

When he didn't travel with the team, he would still do the pre-game show via phone. He would always want to know a couple of things: "What's the lineup?" And, when Piniella was managing the team, "What did Lou say? How did Lou feel?" Every time.

◇◇◇

I scribble down a few notes-substitutions, or lineup changes, or some recent statistic and put it on Post-it® notes so Pat can read them. When I first started the job, I would do the same thing for Ronnie. Ronnie tried to read by osmosis...like if he rubbed it on his eyes, maybe the information would sink in. He'd be holding my note or any other paper or game notes right up against his nose-right up against his eyes. Things would be going on with the game while he was doing this—guys flying around the bases, knocking balls out. Pat would look over wondering why he wouldn't get any reaction out of Ronnie—it was because he was reading a note I had given him. One time, after the inning ended, Pat calmly said to me, "Judd, if you'd like something read on the air, why don't you just give it to me, and I'll make sure it gets done." Finally, I would never give Ronnie anything to read.

When he was unable to travel with us, Ronnie would come on the pre-game show via phone. That was always fun and we would do an opening segment. I'd usually throw Ronnie a zinger right at the end, "Hey, what uniform are you wearing while you're watching the game?" "Well, I sweat a lot, and I have to change my underwear during games, so I'm just wearing a T-shirt and jeans." You just never knew what was going to come out. It was all so much fun.

Opening Day of 2010, the Cubs were playing the Braves. Just getting ready to start the pre-game show. I came on with, "Dazzling blue skies, full stadium here at Turner Field. We've got bunting along the façade, and the Cubs are about ready to start the 2010 campaign with a lot of promise this year. Ronnie, are you excited to get things going?" He says, "Did you do something to my headset? I can't hear. Why can I not hear? I can hear you just fine, but I can't hear me. Is this me?" *This is all on the air.* "This is you right here. How does this sound, Ronnie?" "Good, perfect." "Ronnie are you excited about the season?" "Oh yeah, I'm very excited. I feel like this is going to be the year."

A lot of awkward conversations took place on the air. I would not go out to Arizona at the start of spring training to help Ronnie record interviews, so he was on his own. That was usually a recipe for disaster. The first day, Ronnie is supposed to interview Lou and Larry Rothschild. Before we start the pre-game show, he's supposed to send those in. We're listening to these things and they are badly distorted. I actually had to call over my boss to ask if we could air what he had sent. I was told we could air Rothschild but not Lou. We mentioned to Ronnie that we could not air one of the interviews so, "You and I will just talk through one of the segments and then we'll air the Rothschild interview like we normally would." Ronnie yelled back at me, "I sent those interviews in. I did them, and they were fine. I don't understand what the problem is." This is all off-air.

Now, we start, "Today it's going to be the Cubs and the White Sox from Mesa. Ronnie, Carlos Silva is making his spring training debut with the Cubs." Instead of talking about Silva, he screams out, "I sent both interviews in, and they were fine. I don't understand what the problem is. I did both the interviews and they were fine." This was on the air at the first spring training broadcast his last year.

I said, "Ronnie, we're going to hear from Larry Rothschild a little bit later, and then we're going to talk through the segment with Lou. You can give me what Lou had to say in our next segment." "Oh, okay, all right. Silva is on the mound today, and we're going to see how he looks." We go to break. The assistant program director walks in and says to me, "I think you just had an 'off-air' conversation on the air!"

◇◇◇

My first year on the gig, I remember when we worked at **DODGER STADIUM*** for the first time. I walked into the booth and saw Bill Murray and his brother, Brian, and Brian's wife. Bill was talking to Pat and Ron. I was in awe. Here's one of the greatest performers of all time, and he is just shooting the breeze with Ronnie like he's a little kid.

Ronnie was Cubs 24-hours-a-day. The Cubs were his drug. No matter how Ronnie felt, physically or mentally, as soon as he walked into the ballpark or walked into the clubhouse, his day completely changed. It was like a panacea for him. He would come alive at the ballpark and in the clubhouse—he loved it. He was a ballplayer to the day he died. I have no idea what he was wearing in his casket, but I wouldn't be surprised if it were his uniform.

We would go out to dinner, and he would talk about whatever you would want—family, entertainment...but the Cubs were what he wanted to talk about all the time.

*DODGER STADIUM—since the day it opened in 1962—is the only current stadium that has never changed its seating capacity. Because of a conditional use permit from the city of Los Angeles, the capacity is always 56,000....Fenway Park's seating capacity is lower for day games (36,984) than for night games (37,400).

The blood was blue. Cubbie blue. Ronnie would prick himself all the time to test his blood. I never looked...but I think it came out blue.

Ronnie would always pay the bill wherever we would go. You could never go out to dinner or for drinks, and pay. If you picked up the bill or ever wanted to pay for your share, or tried to throw in cash to defray the cost-oh, he'd get mad. If you were out with Ronnie, Ronnie picked up the tab.

One time, we were in Texas. We were in Lou's office and Ronnie seemed down. Lou asked him, "Hey, Ronnie what's the matter?" Ronnie's stepdaughter Kelly was getting married and they were making wedding and honeymoon plans. Ronnie had mentioned that the place she wanted to go was pricey! Ronnie's wife called him *cheap*. He was absolutely livid. "You're calling me cheap? I'm cheap? You're sitting on a brand new deck with a waterfall behind you in my backyard and you're calling me *cheap*?" It really burned him up. He told Lou, "She called me cheap!"

> We got a chance to work with Pat and Ron—it was a treat every day.

It's really hard to do a baseball schedule if you don't have terrific guys to work with. We got a chance to work with Pat and Ron—it was a treat every day. Just hanging out with those guys in the booth. It was all so much fun. Everything was great—riding with Ronnie to the airport, hanging out with them on the plane. Ronnie sat in first class, probably because there was more room for his legs. Pat would sit with the rest of us.

Ronnie was genuine. I think that's what sticks out for me. It's not only who Ronnie was but the fact that he was so genuine. The man was real. When you come across someone who is genuine, and then combine that with a type of charisma which Ronnie had, and then you pair him with Pat Hughes—with his sense of timing and wit and artistry—that's what you've created. You've created the Pat and Ron Show.

Chapter Seven

SANTOPALOOZA

If a Baseball Could Talk,
It Would Sound Like Ron Santo

WEAK END AT BERNIE'S

LINDA DILLMAN

Dillman was Ron Santo's former personal secretary and a close friend since his early playing days. She is the owner of Bernie's Tavern, an establishment right across the street from Wrigley Field—a popular hangout for Cubs fans.

Ron was amazing. Right now I own a bar—Bernie's—on the corner of Clark and Waveland, two doors down from a gas station where Ron used to park his car. Ron never got in his car and pulled away while there was one person waiting for an autograph. He didn't care how many people would be surrounding his car when he came out. They would walk down the street with him and walk over to where his car was parked, and he would sit in that lot and sign every single autograph request.

I grew up across the street from the ballpark, and my mom was a cashier at Wrigley. She told me the Cubs were needing a bookkeeper, so I went for an interview and got the job—I was 18 years old. A few months later, I met Ron Santo, and had a life-long friendship with him.

I grew up very poor, never had been out of Chicago to go anywhere. I began working at the ballpark when I was 18. In June, a couple of the girls—the switchboard operator and a secretary—were going to take a trip to Cincinnati, and they invited me to go with them. They were going to drive so it wouldn't cost a lot of money, so I went with them to watch the Cubs play. We were having breakfast in Cincinnati and Ron knew the switchboard operator so he saw her and came over to say hi. She introduced me to Ron. We made small talk, "How long have you worked there?" Then, he picked up our breakfast check...I thought that was the most amazing thing in the world.

I didn't know him as being a shy, quiet person from Seattle coming to Chicago. But I also never knew him as thinking he was a ballplayer and a superstar. He was one of the most genuine people I ever met.

> He picked up our breakfast check...I thought that was the most amazing thing in the world.

Now when I look back on things and the friendships I had, sometimes you can just talk to somebody and you know you're just getting a 'conversation,' but other times you can realize you are going to have a friendship. That's how I felt with Ron from day one.

Ron talked about his wife and talked about his children. He said it was always his dream to sign with the Cubs. He was happy that he was in Chicago. He talked about how proud his mother was of him and he hoped one day I would have the privilege of meeting her. It was all amazing to me.

I was still working for the Cubs when they had "Ron Santo Day" at Wrigley Field. His mom and his stepdad were there. He made a point of calling the office and asking if they would allow me to come down by the clubhouse because he had people there he would like for me to meet. They did allow me to go down so I met his mother and stepdad and talked to them for a long time. They allowed me to sit in the dugout, knowing that Ron and I were friends. By then, I had started helping him with his fan mail and correspondence. I had a perfect view sitting in the dugout watching the ceremony on the field. There was a party that night, and I sat and talked with his mother for the longest time.

My father-in-law, Bernie, owned the bar at the time Ron was parking his car at the gas station. My husband and I married, and my father-in-law wanted to retire so all of his kids went into equal partnership and took over the bar. I have two adult sons.

It's like Ron Santo almost took a place as a father figure in my boys' lives. They loved to go on a road trip. Part of being on a road trip with him when he was an announcer was going to the games. Then we would always meet Ron afterward. If it had been a day game, we'd go out and have dinner and a drink with him. We'd meet him after a night game and have a drink with him. He'd sit and talk baseball. My youngest son is so knowledgeable about baseball and that's due to all those conversations with Ron.

He came in after he went over to Wrigley Field one day. He wanted to go into the back room of the bar and talk. He never called me by my maiden name—I was always Dillman to him. He said, "Dillman, let me ask you a question and promise me you'll be honest with me." I'm like, "Nothing but. You've got it." "Did you ever think I could be an announcer?" I asked, "What are you talking about?" He told me about the opportunity and how he would love to do it. I told him, "Your heart has always been in the game, and I think any capacity that you could find yourself being there is where you truly belong." He agreed with me. He said, "You're right. My heart's never left this game." He always used the phrase with me, "I bleed Cubbie blue."

I really truly believe that his being in baseball as long as he was prolonged his life. I most definitely think that announcing for the Cubs kept him alive and gave him a reason.

I remembered JDRF honoring him, and I was invited to be with his family at that ceremony. John McDonough, who was with

JDRF—not the Blackhawks' John McDonough—introduced him, and Ron got a standing ovation. It was amazing. He goes, "Oh my God. If I knew that I would get this much attention, I'd get rid of my other leg." He said that as a joke. But, then he called me up from Arizona and told me what was about to happen again—amputation of the other leg. He never pitied himself. He never felt sorry for himself. It was never, "Why me? Why did this happen to me?" It was always "There's a reason why this happened. God and God alone knows the reason. I'm still alive, and I can still cheer for my Cubs. I still have my family. I have all the things that are really truly important." It was his attitude about everything that he was grateful and happy for every good thing that he had in his life.

In 2010, I knew that the cancer had come back. He called me to tell me that. Naturally I started crying on the telephone, and *he was trying to comfort me*—trying to make me feel better, if that makes any sense. He said, "Dillman, knock it off. Stop it."

It bothered me tremendously. He told me how he could tell his body was feeling different. Amazingly, on that last Tuesday night, his son, Jeff, was with him there and they had watched a movie together in the hospital. Jeff phoned to tell me he was there and that he was leaving. "I called to tell you that Dad says 'Hi.'" I told him," "Tell my pal I said 'Hi,' and I love him, and I'll talk to him soon." He told Jeff to tell me that if everything went right, they were going to let him go home the next day. Then, the next thing I know Jeff calls me and tells me that he was in a coma....

Jeff Santo did that documentary *This Old Cub*. Ron wasn't afraid to lay in the hospital and show himself. He handled that with the class that he was. We were at Wrigley Field the day they were shooting one of the last scenes where they show Ron with his leather Cub jacket on, walking down the line. Ron goes, "Dillman, do me a favor and go over to Bernie's and get me a bite to eat. I need something to eat right now." I quickly got him a candy bar so he would have something to eat immediately. Then I went over to the bar and got a sandwich and brought it back to him. He stumbled, and, even with everything I had in my hands, I grabbed onto his jacket and twisted my hand around it to hold him up. He was fine then, and Jeff walked up to me afterward and said, "If you hadn't done that, and he would have gone down, this whole documentary would have been over."

The day his number was retired, I talked to him when he left his house. He asked me if I was going to be at the ballpark, and I told him, "You know where I'll be, pal." Before he ever said it on the field, from the bottom of my heart, I can tell you, "Dillman, we've talked about me. We've talked about the Hall of Fame. We've talked about everything. But, I will tell you that this totally is my Hall of Fame. It means more to me than that possibly could."

I remember him calling me one day on the way home from a game. He said, "Dillman, the best thing just happened to me that could have happened to me. It put me on a roller coaster so high I don't know if I'll ever come off." I asked him, "What are you talking about?" He said, "John McDonough, the Cubs vice-president, just told me that as long as he is with the Cubs, no one will ever put on **THE #10 UNIFORM***. Do you know how much that means to me?"

To meet someone and have them tell you about their family— Ron's wife who was the mother of his children, Judy—and of being high-school sweethearts. Talking about Ron, Jr. being born and Jeff being born and then when Linda was born. He was at the hospital with his wife and called up and was ecstatically screaming into the phone, "I have a daughter. I have a daughter." He was so happy.

*Santo wore #17 in his first spring training with the Cubs and started wearing #10 in 1960. Billy Grabarkewitz was the first to wear #10 in 1974 after Santo left for the White Sox. When Santo made his debut on June 26, 1960 in Pittsburgh, he wore #15, which actually belonged to Sammy Taylor who was on the disabled list at the time.

I asked him if they had a name for her, and he said, "It's a name you'll never forget as long as you live. Her name's Linda." I go, "Okay, you're right. I'll never forget that one."

The day I heard about Ron's death, I went over to Bernie's to see how the news was being received in the Wrigley Field area. Years ago, when the Cubs first sold the commemorative bricks, I bought Ron a brick the very first year. It said, "Thanks forever friend," signed "Dillman." It's on Addison toward Sheffield. It used to be right on Clark and Addison, but they moved things around because of adding Ernie's statue. This sounds dumb, but the day Ron Santo died my two sons and I went over to the brick and we leaned over and kissed the brick. I told him, "I'll love you forever, pal."

> ... the day Ron Santo died my two sons and I went over to the brick and we leaned over and kissed the brick.

When we went over to the brick, there were 50 or 60 others there. I stayed around the bar for a little bit, and I would walk back down there, and there would be another 20 or so there. Someone had put up a hat and someone had hung his shirt up. It was a constant flow of people the whole day.

I can say truly, from the bottom of my heart, that I did consider Ron Santo my very best friend in the whole world. I could call him up. There were some times and so many instances of things, and it didn't matter what time of day or night that if I needed to talk or whatever, he was always there for me—always.

CHICAGO HOPE

RAY MCKINNEY

McKinney is president of McKinney Prosthetics in Gurnee, IL. He brought so much relief to Ron Santo that Santo and friend John McDonough bankrolled the move of McKinney's business from Scottsdale to the Chicago area.

I first met Ron through his Scottsdale physician in 2001. We had developed a new technology at the time. His physician told me he had patients who had the problem we were talking about. It couldn't have been a week later that he called, "Ray, you're a Chicago boy?" I said, "Yeah." He said, "Northwestern?" I said, "Yes." He asked me, "Are you familiar with Ron Santo?" I said, "Oh, yeah, everyone is."

He asked me if I could meet Ron at the Scottsdale office the next morning. Ron had recently had his leg amputated. He told me Santo had an ulcer on the bottom of his limb. He said he thought it was from pressure when he was in the hospital. I said, "I know it was."

Ron came in, I looked at the wound and told him I had seen this many times before.... "What we're going to do for you will have that healed up in approximately seven days." Ronnie has told this story many times that he thought I was either crazy or very confident...and he was banking on 'confident.'

Primarily, he had shrinkage in the remainder of the limb. Once it shrinks, it starts sliding up and down inside that prostheses causing friction sores, pain and perspiration collection. I sat down and explained to him why he was having those problems and what we would do with a new one to take care of them. He told me to go ahead and "make it today." I told him I couldn't do it that day, that I would have to order components in, and could have it the next day. He told me that he had to go with the Cubs at 11:30 to L.A. I told him that wouldn't be a problem and to just be there by eight o'clock, and I'd have him out the door.

Normally when you would get an old conventional leg like that, it would take two-three weeks to make. With the technique we have today, it's two-three hours. I told him we would have it fabricated for him. He said, "That's impossible." I assured him we could do it.

> He had a driver with him carrying his old prostheses. Ron was hopping on his one leg, using a walker.

He came in the next morning. He had a driver with him carrying his old prostheses. Ron was hopping on his one leg, using a walker. He sat down. I took the cast and fabricated the prosthesis, and by eleven o'clock, he was walking out of the office on two legs. His driver still was carrying that old prostheses.

I got a phone call from him later that afternoon. He said, "Ray, I was able to go to the airport and walk out to the plane, and it didn't hurt. I could sit and it didn't hurt. That may not sound like much to you, but whenever I'd get to the airport, I was always in so much pain I would have to take a wheelchair to get to the gate. But, today I could walk right to the gate. I could bend my knee, and it didn't hurt. I couldn't even feel it. I just thought you'd want to know that."

He called me five days after the sitting and said, "Ray, I've got great news." He said, "It's healed." That whole thing that was quite large—the ulcer—was down to maybe the diameter of a pencil lead. He said, "You told me it might take a week or two, and this is only five days."

Ronnie referred John McDonough to see me—not the John McDonough of the Cubs and Blackhawks fame, but the John McDonough with JDRF (Juvenile Diabetes Research Foundation). John flew out to Arizona the next day. We made the limb, he flew to **SCOTLAND*** for the next 10 days and went golfing.

This certainly is not funny, but it is a very touching story. We had a little boy who was about 10 years old, named Mersim from Croatia. He had only been in the U.S. about four years. He didn't speak English when he first got here. He had horrible health problems so he was in bed a lot. He listened to the radio constantly.

Well...he fell in love with Ronnie and the Cubs. He learned to speak, not only through the community but listening to the radio all the time. He has quite a knack for stats, and it turns out he knew more on the stats of each one of these Cubs players than Ronnie did—or Pat even. Now that's saying something because Pat knows everything—at least Ronnie told me he knew more than Pat. I don't know if that's true. I'd have a hard time believing it.

I set it up for Mersim to go on down to the ballpark with tickets for the game. Ronnie took him up to the booth for a while, took him down on the field, took him into the dugout. He met Sammy Sosa and some of the other players at that time. Mersim thought he won the lottery! It was just the most important day of his life. Three days later his mom went in to get him, and he had passed away in the night, but he had Ronnie's ball in his arms. That touched Ronnie quite a bit. True story, even though it seems like a scene from a **BABE RUTH*** movie.

---

*Only three people have ever appeared on **SCOTLAND**'s five-pound note: Queen Elizabeth II, the Queen Mum, and Jack Nicklaus.

---

*In **BABE RUTH**'s first major league game—as a pitcher for the Boston Red Sox—he was removed in the 7th inning for a pinch hitter.

One day I got the phone call from Ronnie. He said, "Ray, they want to amputate the second leg. Do you have any patients who wear two of them?" I told him, "Ronnie, I must have at least 50. Believe me, you will be just fine." He said, "Well, now my good leg is my prosthetic leg 'cause the heel has gone bad on my real leg. Will the other one be just like this where I can get up and can walk with no pain?" I told him, "Absolutely." He said, "How long would it take?" I told him that after the surgery, we would probably have him walking in three weeks, maybe four, depending on healing. He asked when he could start walking, and I told him right then and there, "Just like we got you going with the other one."

He told me that when the doctors came in, they wanted to try to save it. This was around Thanksgiving. He wanted to be back to spring training in February. The doctors told him they would know by June if they could save it, but by June, he would have missed spring training—he's not in the booth with the boys—he might even lose his job, which he doesn't even want to entertain. He asked the doctors, "What are the odds you can save this foot for me?" The doctors told him 65%. Ron told them, "You gave me 95% on my first, and we still amputated—take it off!"

Later, I flew from Chicago to Scottsdale to change his cast. He said, "Ray, you don't mind if some guys take some pictures, do you?" I told him that would be fine. I got into the office half hour later—a small office—and here are these large booms and banks of lights and microphones. There had to be a dozen or more people running around in my office who normally aren't there—a lot of people. After the hoopla calmed down, and we shut the door with just Ronnie and me in the room, I said, "Ronnie, what is going on?" He said, "We sold the rights to my life story to **TOM HANKS***. One of the camera crews is his."

*__TOM HANKS__ was a soda pop vendor for two years at Oakland A's games...M.C. Hammer was once an A's bat boy and Debbi Fields of Mrs. Fields cookie fame was a ball girl for the A's.

They wanted a shot when Ronnie was getting up to start walking so they would have it for historical accuracy. The other camera crew was his son, who was deciding whether or not he was going to do a documentary movie.

I took the cast for the leg—I do these in about two hours—and went back into my office to make it with the camera crews watching me and filming me as I'm making it. I remember my tech coming up and whispering in my ear, "Ray, are you feeling any pressure now?" I said, "No, I do the same thing for Ronnie, I'd do for anybody, really." The bottom line was when we put on the new prosthetic, and now he has two for the first time. He stood up and walked. There weren't any second takes. There wasn't any practice. That was it. He put those legs on, and he got up to walk, took a few steps back and forth, and after that it was pretty much, "Get out of my way—I'm going."

Ron was back to spring training in February with no problem and never missed a beat. He could still golf. He could still ride his horse. He could do whatever he wanted to do when he was feeling well. There will never be another Ron Santo!

MOVIN' ON UP: FROM THE WHITE SOX TO THE GLENVIEW SOFTBALL LEAGUE

TOM LILL

Lill is a property manager in the Glenview area. The Northern University and DePaul graduate fondly remembers his first meeting with Ron Santo.

There was a softball team that Ron played on after he was done with the White Sox in '74. My neighbor, Dave, had a **SOFTBALL*** team in the Glenview Thursday Night League. Ron's company wanted to sponsor that team. I told Dave to ask Ron if he wanted to play because we were always coming in second to another team that wasn't really that good. We really needed a shortstop. Ron said "yes." I told Dave that if Santo was really serious about it, we'd have to come up with $125 to add his name to the roster. It was only a couple of days later that Dave came by my house and dropped off a $125 check written by Ron Santo. I couldn't believe it was true. I almost felt like keeping the check just for his signature. It was a godsend. I called each of the teammates up to tell them that it was official—he was going to play with us. They were all yelling "I can't believe it! Ron Santo! Ron Santo of the Chicago Cubs!"

---

* In 2012, **SOFTBALL** will be the first sport in 70 years to be eliminated from the Olympic Games.

I can't tell you how much fun that was dialing each of these guys up.

> I almost felt like keeping the check just for his signature.

The first time he showed up, we were already practicing. He had a Lincoln Continental with an "RS 10" license plate. Just to see that thing pull up—I was just a college kid. When he was walking to the softball field, I was in shock! Everybody huddled around and introduced themselves to him and Ron then asked which position everyone played. When he came to me, I said, "Third base." He said, "Third base?" I said, "Yeah." He said, "I always wanted to play shortstop." Whether it was practice or at a game, I always had to look to the left of me to see if it was true. It was true. He was playing shortstop and I was playing third base. This went on for the two years that we played together.

It was hard for him to adjust to softball bats. At the particular time, though, you were allowed to use a hardball bat if the other team agreed. Some of the teams would agree to let him use the hardball bat, but some of the teams wouldn't because it would give him an advantage. He hit about five home runs. They were towering balls—you knew where they were going. He was an excellent fielder and great fun to play with. He caught a couple of times, and he'd stay post-game for just an hour or so. Not every game—just a couple of times to get to know the team better. Crowds of people would converge on him and talk to him—asking him questions. He would never exclude you. If you were in a conversation with him and he was interrupted, he'd always get back to you.

Back in 1975 this happened in the first inning of the first game and the first batter. In fact, Glenn Beckert and his wife were also there. A lot of Glenview residents had seen a story in the Glenview newspaper that he was playing softball. The stands were filled. We were playing the number-one rated team. The first batter hit a ground ball sharply to Ron's right. Ron picked it up gracefully, as usual, which I had seen hundreds of time on TV. But, he threw the ball way over the first baseman's head, just below the top row of the grandstand. Ron's standing there as I'm walking toward him. He's shaking his right hand in a scolding way saying, "Damn it! Damn it! I'm gripping it like a baseball." I gave him some advice that I had learned when I was ten years old in a baseball school. I said, "Next time that you catch the ball, take a step or two towards first base and flip it with your wrist until you can adjust." I remember vividly Ron saying, "I'll do that." Imagine me telling a major league all-star and captain and he's going to take my advice? I was on cloud nine.

The third base coach of the opposition shouts, "Hey, big man, you stink!" Ron, without hesitation, shoots back, "Hey, you're ugly!" First, I looked at this guy in shock and then quietly told this guy to "Shut the ---- up!" The game, thankfully, resumed without any further incidents. Our team prevailed in a 5—4 victory that ended with a couple of their runners on base. As customary, in a display of good sportsmanship, each team would line up for the congratulatory handshake with comments like "nice catch," "nice hit," "nice play," etc. But, only nine out of ten of their players shook hands with us. One of their players was missing, and one of the players on our team noticed that—Ron Santo. Next we all heard Ron yell over to the opposition's bench, "Hey, Ugly, nice game!" Everyone then focused on that one big-mouth guy, "Ugly", who was spotted with his head down in a dejected way. What makes the story even better and more memorable is that the guy really was ugly.

When my mom died in 1977, I wasn't playing softball with him but he even came to my mom's wake. He was just such a thoughtful guy. To have a major league baseball player play 16-inch softball was an honor, let alone to have someone like Ron Santo play and to be teammates with him was just unbelievable. I played fourteen years in that league. But, nothing ever surpassed that two years of playing with Ron. I played a game or two with Glenn Beckert which was also neat. Ron had a golf game on a particular day and there was something wrong with his hand, too. It was Saturday afternoon so he had Glenn Beckert play short center in place of him and he placed me at shortstop in place of himself.

Listening to Ron for the last ten years, I felt badly for him because his responses weren't like I remembered him. When I played ball with him, his responses were very quick and poignant. In his commentaries, his pace had slowed most likely due to all his medical challenges and it saddened me, even though his immediate reactions to the game were the same as how most Cub fans reacted (i.e. "Oh, no!" "I can't believe it!"). Many times I would tell my friends that that is not the way he talked when I knew him. If he only spoke a few words, they were forceful, meaningful in tone and content—great qualities of a leader and a captain for a professional baseball team.

I have wonderful memories of Ron Santo.

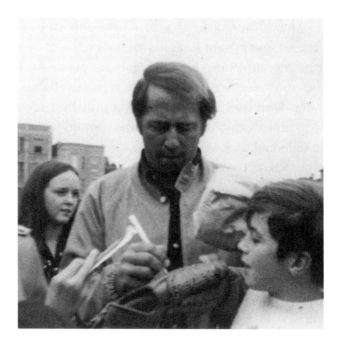

RON SANTO WAS GOD'S WAY OF BEING NICE TO CHICAGO

SUELLEN JOHNSON

Suellen Johnson joined the Juvenile Diabetes Research Foundation, as a volunteer, in 1975 when her 4-year-old daughter was diagnosed with juvenile diabetes. In 1979, Suellen and her late husband, Ted, helped launch the Ron Santo Walk for Diabetes Research. The Johnson family continues to be involved with the Walk and other JDRF efforts to find a cure for diabetes.

I first met Ron Santo when four of us sat down with him at the Lilac Lodge in Hillside, IL in March, 1979 to discuss the possibility of him lending his good name to a fundraising walkathon that we wanted to start for the Juvenile Diabetes Foundation.

Prior to the March, 1979 luncheon I asked a friend what Ron Santo looked like because I didn't know how I would identify him at the restaurant. I grew up as a **MILWAUKEE BRAVES*** fan. A friend said that he was short and stocky and possibly had thinning hair; so I stood at the front door of the Lilac Lodge watching all of the short, stocky, balding men in gray pinstriped suits come in for lunch, wondering which of them might be Ron. Fortunately, when the trim guy with a crew cut wearing Levis, a bright ski jacket and penny loafers walked in, one of my JDRF

*Phil Niekro was the last active former **MILWAUKEE BRAVES** player to play in the big leagues....Niekro lost only one game in high school. The winning pitcher was Bill Mazeroski...Niekro grew up directly across the street from John Havlicek.

colleagues arrived at the same time and indicated that the young guy in the ski jacket was Ron. Embarrassment averted.

Ron was initially reluctant to get involved in a walkathon; I think because he felt it was too self-serving. After all, he was the one with the disease. We explained that we understood that he did not need the cure, but our children did. With that, he signed on and jumped in with both feet. For the next thirty-two years he was there for us. When Ron Santo committed to something, he committed 100 percent. He encouraged our children at the first Ron Santo Walk Kickoff event, he posed for photos with children with diabetes from 35 different Chicagoland communities, he solicited friends for prizes and donations, he did the talk show circuit to promote the Walk, he taped public service announcements, he did everything we asked and more. The day of the first Walk, he walked a portion of the 20 kilometers and signed the T-shirts of all 1,000 walkers. He was the celebrity name behind the Walk but he also was a full partner in promoting and producing the 1979 Walk and every Walk since; with his involvement increasing with each passing year, rather than decreasing as one might have expected.

... when he was speaking with a young person, he was NOT to be interrupted for anything.

Thanks to Ron's good name, the Walk grew in size but really took off when Ron joined the WGN radio family in 1990. The publicity from WGN and the Cubs organization helped us to take giant steps forward and the Walk now raises $5-$6 million each year—the largest fundraiser that JDRF hosts nationwide. Ron would visit two or three Walk sites each year and spend several hours at each site. He would sign autographs and listen to stories from children with diabetes, from their parents and from frustrated Cubs fans. And when he was speaking with a young person, he was NOT to be interrupted for anything.

Ron was a hero to many. It meant the world to young children to know that someone who had the same disease that they had was once a professional baseball player. The kids would come with their baseball gloves and baseballs for him to autograph. One of my daughter's prized possessions from 1979 is her baseball glove that reads, "Congratulations on doing your own shot. Your friend, Ron Santo." Parents (women and men) of young children would look Ron in the eye and say, "Ron, I love you." He really meant the world to parents. The fact that he would give so much of himself was just unbelievable. It was an honor and very moving to work with Ron at every Walk for 32 years and observe the admiration that people felt for him. And how great it was that people expressed it directly to Ron. I don't think it ever occurred to any of us that one day he would not be here. Fortunately, people did not wait to express their admiration, appreciation and love for him. Each year he would counsel young children to take good care of themselves and that everything would be okay. As he stood there with both legs amputated (not to mention the numerous laser treatments on his eyes and all of his heart problems) he would assure them that what happened to him would not happen to them, thanks to advances in diabetes management and research. He was determined to be a positive role model despite the enormous setbacks he had suffered. He was our hero.

In addition to the Walkathon, Ron was involved in many other JDRF events. As he became more conversant in diabetes research issues, he agreed to testify before Congress on behalf of increased diabetes research at the National Institute of Health. The first time he testified in the early 1980's before the House Appropriations Committee, he had an insulin reaction (low blood sugar) right before it was time for him to testify. In typical Ron Santo fashion, he had arrived at O'Hare early. He had done his insulin before he left home and did not eat much on the plane, despite my concern. When someone with diabetes injects insulin, they must eat soon after or they risk a low blood sugar problem. So, sure enough, before he could testify,

I was running around a cavernous House Office Building on the Hill trying to find orange juice, soda, a candy bar—anything that would help bring his blood sugar up. He drank a quart of orange juice and then went into the hearing. The staff members said he was the best celebrity witness they had ever had. Laughing, Ron said he didn't remember a thing he said. He just kept remembering that he was supposed to thank them for last year's appropriation and then ask for more. He always joked about not being a serious student but the truth was he was very fast on his feet; he knew how to do a presentation and could make a great speech, without notes. He spoke from his heart.

On one of his trips to Washington, D.C. for JDRF, Ron met Congressman Silvo Conte, of Massachusetts, a fellow Italian. For the record, I would like to point out that Ron was actually half Italian and half Swedish. I once found a paperback in which the author said that Ron's temperament came from the Italian side but his good looks came from the Swedish side. He borrowed the book and I never got it back. But I digress. On the trip where he met Silvo, a mutual admiration was established. Congressman Conte, who was very important to JDRF's Hill efforts because he sat on the important Appropriations Committee, told Ron he wanted Ron to go on a fishing trip with him to Alaska. Ron, who loved warm climates, came out of the meeting and declared, "You know I will do anything for JDRF, but I am NOT going fishing in Alaska."

In addition, Ron was involved in numerous JDRF Man-of-the-Year Dinners in Chicago. These are annual fundraising dinners. Ron was involved with dinners honoring Mike Ditka, **MICHAEL JORDAN***, Phil Jackson, Ryne Sandberg, Harry Caray and, of course, Ron himself. With each of the dinners, Ron was very particular about the food that was served—it was not to be

---

*In 1994, the White Sox recalled **MICHAEL JORDAN** from Double-A Birmingham to play against the Cubs in the Mayor's Trophy Game at Wrigley Field. Jordan singled and doubled against the Cubs.

rubber chicken. And he was particular about the program. It was to be meaningful—not long, and everything was to run on time. He was involved in the videos that were produced for each dinner and basically paid attention to every detail. At the JDRF *Harry Caray, 50 Years in Baseball Celebration,* Ron got on the microphone before dinner and called me to the podium. I figured it must be important as I dashed to the front. When I got near him, Ron ordered me to, "Take Harry to the bathroom." Ron wanted Harry escorted so that Harry wouldn't be diverted and everything would continue to run on time.

As if Ron had not already done enough to raise money for diabetes research, he started the Ron Santo Golf Classic. The event has raised many more millions for research.

Just as in 2003, when Ron knew he was facing bladder cancer— on October 3, 2010 when he left the Walk to head for Arizona the next day, he never mentioned that he was not feeling well and that he had a check-up scheduled for October 11, the day after son Jeff's 10/10/10 wedding. While many of us regret not having closure with Ron, we have to be at peace knowing that #10 did it his way. Ron's family has agreed that his legacy will continue, and they will be there for future Ron Santo Walks.

LEVEL WITH US RONNIE OR WE'LL PULL THE RUG OUT FROM RIGHT OVER YOU

After Ron lost his first leg, he hit a slump in his wardrobe. It was difficult to change. He wore jeans all the time. For a couple of years, he went into the pants that were easy to get on and off—the nylon type pants. I told him that look was just not cutting it. I found a place that had Levis, which he loved. I showed him some that had some stretch to them so he could get the feet through them. He thought that was cool. I found some Robert Graham shirts that the ballplayers wore.

I told him, "We're doing a total makeover with you...so the next move is to find you a good hairpiece." He wore the *worst* hairpiece for 28 years. I found a guy who did hairpieces for him that were phenomenal—really awesome. Ron would put them on and then would say to me, "HOW DOES IT LOOK?" But...he would never comb the back. I'd go, "Ron, the front is fine—but the back...looks terrible." He'd put it on and then he'd come to me and ask how it looked. I'd always have to tweak it a little. It would be a little lopsided or a little to the left or a little to the right. I wanted to stay out of that because I knew if I took that over, I'd be putting it on him every day.

Ron didn't have a lot of patience, and the guy who made the hairpieces was very busy. So, he went to a girl who had been coloring his hair for him. She colors it and matches his hair to the hairpiece but she doesn't know anything about hairpieces so she blow-drys it *backward!* Hairpieces have a front to them and a back to them. He came home...*with the hairpiece on backward...* but he doesn't know it's on backward. I looked at him and knew something was really wrong. I look at the front and thought it looked like the shingle on a roof that was laying down forward, but, I couldn't say anything...so he wore it like that for three days.

Finally, we were going out with a group of people and Ron wanted to really look good so he said he was going to wear his "#1 hairpiece." He puts it on and goes, "There's something wrong. What's wrong with this?" I said, "Probably if we just turn it around, it will look a lot better." He went, "Oh my lord. J---- C-----! I've been wearing it this way for three days." He was so upset. I told him to just wear a hat. He said, "I can't wear a hat where we're going." But, he didn't want to wear the other hairpiece. Finally, he realized he had it on backward and had to rewash it, reblow dry it. He had so many hairpiece stories.

Bald on Ron was not a good look. Right before I met him, he was doing comb-overs. Then, he had a hairpiece, but I don't think he realized it was not that good. The guy who did it did it the same way for 30 years, overcharged him, and I did not think it looked that good. Hairpieces have become really good—where you cannot tell they are hairpieces.

Ron was very vain. He always wanted to look his best, but he had no sense of style as far as how to fix it.

—**VICKI SANTO**, Ron Santo's widow

I didn't know he had a hairpiece. He never said much about it. and I never saw him with it off. He looked fine to me. I thought he looked great.

—**ERNIE BANKS**, Mr. Cub

We used to have fun with his hairpiece. When I was growing up, he and Vicki would go on vacation, I'd stay at their house and watch my sister, Kelly. We'd do all sorts of things—like wear the hair piece around. We made a mock-up guy. We used the Styrofoam head for the hairpiece and put it under a blanket so it looked like there was a man sleeping on the couch if we were scared. Years later my son Sam would just laugh at Dad watching him put on the hairpiece in the morning when he was over there. My dad would do his hair and then do Sam's hair. They never realized until he took his hat off. Spencer said since Grandpa didn't have hair and he didn't have legs that grandpa was a robot. My youngest son Spencer would play with him and step on his feet and Dad would yell "Ouch! You're hurting

my feet!" And, Spencer would jump and say, "What?"—when Spencer couldn't feel his feet because they weren't there.
—**LINDA SANTO BROWN**, Ron Santo's daughter

In late July of 2010, Ron and I were meeting in a conference room of a suburban Chicago hotel. Most conference rooms have huge oak tables. This conference room had a table that, unbeknownst to us, was like a jigsaw puzzle. It locked together underneath, out of sight. Ron is sitting across from me. He leaned back in his chair, cupping both hands behind his head. Suddenly, the chair kept going backward. In a blur, his hands were on the table to stop him from falling. But...because that end of the table was not connected, he kept going, landing hard beneath the table. I jumped up to help him. Ron was upside down—his Cub cap had gone flyin'—his toupee had almost fallen off. It was connected to the nape of his neck by a thin adhesive strip, which meant it was *upside down* and inside out along his spine.

I said, "Ron, are you okay?" He said, "Yeah. I'm fine." He was embarrassed with the toupee hanging down the back of his spine so I said, "Oh, man. Do you mind? I have to go to the bathroom really, really bad." "Oh, no. That would be great. Run along. I'll be fine. Don't worry about me at all. I'm in good shape." I wait in the hallway. About 30 seconds later, Ron appears with his toupee on semi-straight, Cub cap back on, big smile on his face—just like nothing had happened.
—**RICH WOLFE**, Co-author of this book

Ron would get different hairpieces. There were three guys on the ball club at one time who had hairpieces. Kessinger and Pepitone also wore a "piece." The other guys would be styling theirs. Ronnie thought that was a lot of waste of time—blow-drying it, curling it. You had to stick it on with tape, and it had to be on straight. If it wasn't on straight, you looked odd. There were always guys who would go, "Hey, Ronnie, you're making enough money to buy a good hairpiece." "Nah, this looks great. I'm not spending any more money."

Pepitone was the guy who came over in 1970 and his hairpiece was on a Styrofoam head. He would curl it, blow-dry it and put it on. He'd tape front, back, side—all over. It looked like a big helmet he wore. Ronnie had more hair than Peppy. Peppy was almost bald. The same with Kessinger—when he started losing his hair, he had to put a hairpiece on.

The guys would fall asleep on the plane. Santo would wake up and the guys would say, "Ronnie, fix your hairpiece." Ronnie was really sensitive about it. Every man deals with little idiosyncrasies. Losing your hair is a manly thing. When I started losing my hair, I just shaved my head. Some guys don't want to do that, though. Ronnie took pride in fixing his toupee and looking stylish in it. That was part of his makeup.

—**FERGIE JENKINS**, Cubs Hall of Famer

Ron's hairpiece was always on when he came out of his house. I may be one of the few people who actually have seen this but, in the bathroom he had those mannequin heads to hold his wigs. He had three of them. The "#1" was the one he wore most often. The only time he wasn't wearing it and you knew he wasn't wearing it was whenever he was wearing a ball cap. No telling why he didn't have the piece on.

In my ten years of driving Ron, I only saw the man without his hairpiece and without his cap one time. It was a particularly hot summer day and Ron gets in the car. The air conditioner wasn't blowing that well and it was really, really hot. He lifts up the bill of his cap and runs his hand over his bald head and runs his hand through his remaining hair and shakes his hand to get rid of the sweat he had collected and gave a "Whew" and put the cap right back on. I was in the front seat, and he was in the back seat and I saw all of this in my rear view mirror and just about fell out. It was a sight to see. It was scary. It left me jarred the rest of the way. All I could think about was that bald head. "That is NOT the man I know!"

—**TEX REBRESH**, Ron Santo's Driver

We were in St. Louis in 2005. I always had a room next to Ron and had an extra key in case anything happened. I got a phone call from him asking me if I had a baseball hat in my bag and if I did, would I bring it to him in his room. So I thought, "Sure, I'll bring it to you." He answered the door—it was one of two times I've ever seen him without his toupee on. That's a proud man—he didn't like people to see him without his toupee on. He looked at the baseball hat I brought him, and he didn't like it. I asked him, "What's going on?"

He said, "I can't find my hairpiece. I just can't find it. It's got to be in here somewhere, but I can't find it." I decide I will go into his room and help him look for it. We're getting close to the time when we have to go to the ballpark. We're tearing that place apart. I looked in the bathroom. I looked in the shower. I looked in the drawers and in the closet. We tore the bed apart. We were looking underneath the sheets—every place. I couldn't figure out where the heck he could have actually lost this piece of hair.

I had seen a bunch of papers on the desk so I walked over to the pile. I picked up the *USA Today* and was shuffling it around a little bit. There was a sack right on top of a Federal Express box on the desk pushed back by the wall. I was rifling through the papers and there was nothing there.

I picked up this Federal Express box, and attached to the bottom of the Federal Express box, was his toupee. I've got to tell you...it looked like a dead animal...just hanging from the bottom of this box. The glue had caused it to stick to the box. The logical thought was that I would have pulled the hairpiece off the box and taken it over to him, but it looked like something that would bite me so I took him the box to let him take it off the bottom of the box. The look on his face was "You've got to be kidding me." It was right there the whole time! The Cubs had sent him some publicity shots they were giving away at a game in the next home stand. He was signing all those pictures and lost track of where the toupee was. There it was on the bottom of the Federal Express box, and we just died laughing. Ron had this propensity for not remembering things, but yet being good-natured enough to realize that nobody was laughing at him—we were all laughing with him. He had a real good time with us.

We had a lot of discussions on-air about his toupee. He actually had names for all of them. He had three in a set and he rotated them, depending on age of the hairpiece. Number one was always the 'going-out on the town, looking good' toupee. Number two was just a slightly lesser version of number one. Number three was always affectionately known as 'the gamer.' It was only to be worn with a baseball hat. He was so proud of these hairpieces. They were like members of the family.

—**ANDY MASUR**, San Diego Padres announcer,
formerly with the Cubs

You couldn't touch his hair. His hair was everything. He combed his hair, and it had to be a certain way, and that's the way it was. When he started losing his hair, that was tough.

When Ron got the hairpiece, I told him, "I knew right away you were going to do that." I knew how vain Ron was. I knew he never would go without hair. When he played ball, he still had some hair on the sides and always had a ball cap on so normally he wouldn't wear his hairpiece when he played ball. It drove him nuts when he was losing his hair. But, Ron looked good all the time. He must have looked at himself in the mirror about 10-20 times, but he looked good. It's because of that vain part of him. He always—always—took care of himself. It didn't surprise me at all that he got a hairpiece.

Ron was quite a good looking guy. He had this blond, sandy hair. When he was young, it was nice. He wore it the way he wanted to. When he went to get a haircut, he let the barber know exactly what he wanted.

—**ADIELENE SANTO**, Ron Santo's sister

One time Ronnie locked his hairpiece in the hotel and he had to send a representative of the team back to the hotel to get his hairpiece. Of course, there was the time it caught on fire at Shea

Stadium when he stood up for the anthem and got too close to the heaters that were on the ceiling. More than all of that, we used to have a lot of fun taking shots of Ron in the radio booth. Len Kasper would say, "I wonder if Ron is wearing 'his gamer' today." He had different pieces to wear on different occasions. I would always act shocked—"Ron wears a toupee?" Of course, everyone on the face of the earth knew it but I would always act like it was a surprise to me. No matter how many times we would bring it up in the course of the year, I would always act shocked that Ron had a hairpiece.

—**BOB BRENLY**, Cubs TV Broadcaster

Ronnie crashed his Corvette down in Arizona one year. Thankfully he wasn't killed, but he apparently went into a diabetic coma and passed out or got lightheaded. In the crash, somehow the toupee was lifted off the top of his head. They took him to the hospital. When the police and the tow truck came, they were able to retrieve his toupee from out of the car. They restored it and he was able to use it again. It was the first thing he asked for when he woke up.

—**BRUCE MILES**, *The Daily Herald*

My dad passed in 2004, but if he had still been living when I started working for the Cub organization, I would have had to barricade him from the booth. He would have been up there every day. My first year was 2009 and I worked '09 and '10 with Ronnie. My mom, who is also a huge Cub fan still can't believe I work for the Cubs. She thought it was the biggest thing in the world. Actually, she and Ronnie went to the same hair salon. My mom once told me, "Next time you see Ron, ask him about Sheer Elegance, a hair salon in Northbrook. I said, "What?" She said, "Yeah, we go to the same hair salon." So, one day I brought it up with Ronnie, "Do you go to Sheer Elegance?" "I do. That's where I get my hairpiece done." I told him, "My mom goes there." "Oh really?"

He would scream at me, "I hate it when you call it a toupee. It's a hairpiece." He hated the word 'toupee'... why, I have no idea.

One day we were talking about the hairpiece—that topic came up all the time. Ronnie once told me, "You would look awful if you had a hairpiece." "Why? I get the same haircut that you have." "You do not. You would look awful." I shave my head, and Ronnie would ask me all the time, "How often do you shave your head?" "Probably a couple of times a week." "Oh!" He seemed to be fascinated by that.
—**JUDD SIROTT**, Arlington Heights native, Buffalo Grove H.S.

I've heard some of the clips of Harry Caray and some of the other guys tease him about his hairpiece. The one that is the best is the one in Shea Stadium. Ronnie was standing up for the National Anthem. Andy Masur was sitting next to me and Pat and Ron were in front. The first thing I noticed was this burnt smell. My first reaction was, "Oh, no. Our mixer is on fire, or failing, or the equipment is burning." So, I'm looking frantically through the cords and cables. The last thing I thought about was that it could be someone's hair on fire. Sure enough, there's this little billow of smoke coming up and I catch Pat grabbing like a Dixie cup or something with water and he kind of splashes Ron's hair and he's matting it down. I thought, "You've got to be kidding me. That's his hairpiece?" Everyone still laughs about it.

People would ask about Ron's hairpiece. Sometimes Pat Hughes would make up a Fax that made it look like it was from a listener, talking about, "Ronnie, I hear you have a hairpiece. How do you wash it? I have a hairpiece and I suggest running it through the dishwasher. It's fabulous! You're hair is clean and you don't have to worry about drying it." For three or four days, they just kept going with it.

—**MATT BOLTZ**

Always...the best thing about clinching was waiting for Ron to come into the clubhouse...for multiple reasons. First of all because all the players literally knew that when we won the Division, it was bigger to Ronnie than it was to the guys on the field. Then, also there was the excitement of seeing what he was going to do with the champagne going off everywhere—with his interesting hair! What kind of hat he would pull down over his head tightly enough so that his toupee wouldn't be exposed.

He was the only man I ever met in my life who would ask you how the toupee looked. I never saw Ron without the toupee on. It was the worst toupee I had ever seen in my life.

A couple of seasons ago, Ron was trying out different toupees, like people try out cars, he was giving them all a little run. Ron wore one of them for a couple of games and he looked like Rod Stewart. The toupee was spiky and looked like an animal—kind of "porcupiney." It didn't really match the hair that was below it. It made him look younger, but not in a good way. He never suffered from that problem! Stevie Wonder could tell that Ron's hair was not real! He only wore it for a couple of days. At first I thought it was special when he asked me how it looked—I figured that someone wouldn't talk to just anyone about their toupee! But later that day, I found out Ron had pretty much asked everybody he came across in the ball park. So...it wasn't as personal as I had hoped.

Ron's toupee was part of him. It wasn't a sore subject. It wasn't anything he was shy about in any way. Ron would talk about his toupee. He had *a gamer!* The funniest thing was Matt Boltz, his producer/engineer, would have the opportunity to see him without the toupee on. Often the first question we would always ask was, "Did you see Ron without the toupee on?" Maybe it was because the man wore a baseball cap his entire career. It was like he always had to have something on the top of his head.

—**MARC BRADY**, WGN-TV Producer

Ron Santo passed away yesterday. He was 70, his toupee, 30.
    —**CHICAGO WRITER GENE WOJCIECHOWSKI**

SHORT STORIES FROM LONG MEMORIES

When I would get to the ballpark, after I dropped him off, my first order of duty would be to go to the 7-Eleven around the corner to go get a bag of ice and some beer so I would have it in the car. I'd load up six Coors Light into the cooler and top it off with ice. Four-and-a-half hours later, after the game, that beer is super ice cold. On a hot summer day, when Ron would get in the car, the first thing you'd hear was that 'pop' of beer and a big swig, and he'd look over at me and say, "Big Boy, that's good."

When we first started riding together, I had a Town Car so Ron sat in the back seat. We'd talk a little bit here and there but he mostly read the paper. As time went on, and I purchased a new SUV, Ron started riding up front with me, riding shotgun. The paper went down more, and our conversation went up. We talked about everything from baseball to our families to what was going on in our personal lives. Like, if the defibrillator in his chest went off in the middle of the night, Ron would tell me about it. He'd tell me what the jolt was like and how it shot him out of his bed.

Ron was so angry after a Cubs loss that whoever he talked to on the phone—they would catch h---. They might call to ask him what happened. He'd say, "Geez! I don't know what the h--- happened. What are you calling me for?" After the Cubs would lose, he was always p----- off. When I would see him, it would always be right after the game ended and the last couple of years, there were a lot of one-run losses. Those were the worst. Ron absolutely hated that kind of a loss, especially if it was a game when the Cubs were ahead and lost the lead in the late innings. That just tore Ron up.

For Ron, every moment that wasn't one of those angry moments was a happy moment. Lots of things made the guy happy. The fact that he was going to a ballgame when we'd leave the house in the morning made Ron happy. The prospect of a new day—everything. Everything made him happy. Talking on the phone to his daughter, Linda, or talking to his grandchildren. Finding out how they did in that day's baseball game.

Ron Santo was like my brother. He was like my father. He was like my grandfather. He was like my best friend.

—**TEX REBRESH**, Ron Santo's driver the last 10 years of his life

It was a close-knit team. If you look now on that roster, we've lost about 12 guys to the Grim Reaper. The last one before Ronnie was Gene Oliver, Willie Smith, Dick Selma—all the coaches are gone except for Joey Amalfitano. The first guy to die was Hank Aguirre, then Selma. We've lost so many guys off that ball club. We're all circling the drain faster every day.

> Ron Santo was a great ballplayer...and a better person.

I'm happy the Cubs are going to wear #10 on their uniforms. I think it's fabulous for them to do that. Ron was a great, great individual. Ron was the third best third-baseman in National League history—behind Mike Schmidt and Eddie Mathews. The first two guys are in the Hall of Fame, and Ronnie deserves to be in the Hall of Fame. It's too bad he's going to go in posthumously. His boys will represent him, but it's too bad Ronnie didn't have the chance personally to understand that baseball respected for him for his ability. Ron Santo was a great ballplayer...and a better person.

—**FERGIE JENKINS**, 20-game winner

The biggest thrill for me was to fill in for Ron. We became good friends when I did TV, and he was on the radio and we traveled together. The last couple of years, I wouldn't see Ron that much because we weren't traveling at the same time.

It was in '04, the team was on the road in Cincinnati, he was in his hotel room, and his defibrillator went off. He called and asked me if I could go down to Cincinnati to fill in for him. He described what he was going through. Even though he's having this problem, the conversation was the most upbeat you could imagine. He was excited about the way the Cubs were playing. That was Ron in a nutshell. The Cubs were so important to him...and that really drove him.

In '03, he had just lost his second leg, and in the fall, toward the end of the year, I filled in for him when he was going through bladder cancer. The Cubs were five outs away from going into the World Series. That off-season I decided to fly down to Scottsdale to spend a couple of days with a buddy of mine who lives there. That would give me a chance to go to Ronnie's house to see him. My buddy picked me up at the airport so I didn't have a car. I was at my hotel, waiting for my buddy to come so I could drive out to see Ron. Instead, I saw a bus outside the hotel so I decided to take the bus to his house and call a cab to bring me back to the hotel. He lived about 45 minutes away.

I get off where I thought I was pretty close to his house. I call a cab and then I called Ron and told him I was coming over in a little bit. He said, "Okay, Rusty." The cab never showed up so I called him back to tell him I was going to be later because I had to call another cab. He asked me what I was doing that for, and I told him I had taken a bus out to there and then was planning to get a cab. He said, "You TOOK a bus! Rusty, I'll see you in spring training." So, I didn't get to see him that trip.

Ron was so much fun to be around.

—**DAVE OTTO**, whose father Al, in 1966, hit a legendary towering home run at Yankee Stadium that is still much discussed

I got to really know Ron in the early nineties going to the Randy Hundley Cubs Fantasy Camps. At the very first camp, Randy put me with Ron—we knew each other, and we shook hands. We went out the first day. He was trying to work with these older guys who can't play a lick. But, they wanted to be there and have fun so Ron is working with them real seriously. You know how competitive Ron was! While he was working with them, he gets a call that one of his really good friends in Chicago had passed away. He had to leave the camp for a few days.

We had got slaughtered in the first game when Ron was trying to help us. Then, after he left, the next three days we won every game we played in. I was trying to help manage the club and helping to do everything I could. Ron came back, and the others guys and I started ribbing him a little bit. We told him, "Hey, you've got a lot to live up to after what we've done." He was going around working with all the guys, and...well...*we didn't win another game.*

We get to Saturday night at the banquet. We are introducing the players. We said, "When we lost our manager, life became a lot better...we won six ballgames in a row. We did NOT win a game once he came back." I looked at him and said, "Ron, I have a feeling that you don't know a lot about baseball. What are your numbers?" It doesn't sound as good as it was! It was classic in a banquet environment. Ron got a little flustered. It was fun to be involved with him in all that.

Anyone who listened to the Cubs and was a fan of Ron's knew no one wanted the Cubs to win more than Ron Santo. Because of that, I didn't think too much about following Ron as broadcaster for the Cubs. I knew he had some times when he was struggling to get around and at times he had been nice enough to me to ask me to come fill in for him. Being there with Pat, Judd and Matt and everybody was special. They put me under their wings, making me feel very comfortable. I got to fill in a few times.

Then, when we lost Ron, all of us were crushed. I didn't even think about the job at that point and didn't know what decision was going to be made about a broadcaster, so I wasn't even going to inquire about the job. After the first of the year, WGN called me and asked me if I was interested. When I told them I was, they said they didn't even have an application from me. I said, "Out of respect for Ron, I wasn't going to apply until they made an announcement asking for applications." I had stayed out of the mix, and then had the great opportunity of having them choose me. I don't know how lucky I got...but I got lucky.

—BOBBY KEITH MORELAND,
Ron Santo's successor in the broadcast booth

My friend and I used to go out to Chicago see Ron a lot. Early on, when Ron had just signed with the Cubs in his second season, he was really getting into harness racing there in Chicago. We'd go out to the track and sit in the President's Box. Someone would come up and tell us who to bet on. Ron got pretty involved in that. One day after the season was over, Ron came to me and my mother, who was an English teacher. He got a letter from National League President Warren Giles telling him he'd better quit hanging out with these guys because it wasn't good for baseball. Ron wanted my mother and me to help him write a letter back telling them that he would do what they wanted and that would be the end of it. That was it.

He was a pretty religious man. For many, many years, he went to Mass, and he was happy about it. Ron may have been too young when he married Judy. Many nights when the Cubs played the Giants, I drove up. We'd be out until 2-3 in the morning, and there would be a doubleheader the next day. The Cubs would be out playing—going at it, and I was barely alive. I never, never understood how he could do that.

> I took the pin off and gave it to her...and she started crying.

That day of the funeral, after the party at the restaurant, Bill and I were walking back to the hotel and we went into Starbucks. The Cubs organization had given me one of those pins with "10" on them before the funeral. They looked like gold. I had been wearing it on my suit. This woman was sitting there having coffee, and I said to her, "Are you a Cubs fan?" She had Cubs stuff all over her and a lot of Ron Santo garb. She said, "I grew up with the Cubs, and I loved Ron Santo." I took the pin off and gave it to her...and she started crying. That's the love you saw of the general population. I didn't realize it that much until then. This was just a lady in Starbucks, and she had no idea I knew Santo from childhood.

No way would we have known when we knew him early in junior high or high school that he would be the person he turned out to be. Very few athletes from the Seattle area make it to the big time—very few. The funeral was sad, really sad. Healthwise, Ron had a hard life. He was such a fabulous person.

—**JOHN PHILLIPS**, 71, Sun Valley, Idaho—Ron Santo's childhood friend

A former Chicago Cub with a current Chicago bear

WE WON'T BE BACK RIGHT AFTER THIS...

Ronnie was different from the others because he wasn't scripted—he wasn't polished in the sense of being a broadcaster. He never went to a broadcasting school, never took voice lessons. Ronnie was what he was—a kind of audible stream of consciousness on the air. Whatever he felt, you knew it. Error...you heard the groan! Home run...he'd be yelling right along with Pat. Cubs win—Cubs lose...he felt it. I think what made him different was just the fact that he was himself—and himself was good enough. He might not have been the best technical analyst in the game, couldn't break down pitches—he could but he didn't always do it. He could tell you things about why a guy was good, but that wasn't much fun. The more fun part of listening to Ronnie was him conveying his emotions. That's what made him unique. And, the fact that even though he wasn't from Chicago, he became a "Cub." Once he started playing for the Cubs and finished with them—he never counted that year with the White Sox, believe me, he never counted that as a year in baseball—he was a Cub. We had a true-blue Cub in the broadcast booth who related to every man out there.

Ron Santo was a beauty.

—**BRUCE MILES**, *The Daily Herald*

In the fall of 2010, Vicki Santo called to tell me that Ron had been diagnosed with bladder cancer again. She figured he probably would not talk about it in the car as we made our annual rounds to the various Walk sites for JDRF's Ron Santo Walk for the Cure. And she was right, he said very little other than "it will be alright." That day he visited three walk sites, signed hundreds of autographs at each site, took photos with everyone who asked and listened to the stories of his greatest fans, young people with diabetes and their parents. Never once would you have known that the next day he would head to Arizona for surgery and would die in less than 60 days. He listened to the concerns of young children and was his usual upbeat self, especially about the Cubs. I stood in awe of him many times but never more so than on that day. As he got in the car to drive home, I just shook my head in wonder at the strength and determination of that third baseman who focused on everyone else but himself. A true team captain.

—**SUELLEN JOHNSON**, JDRF Volunteer

I'm not a person with a cell phone that pushes a fast-dial button to call somebody—I want to dial the number because then I know I will remember it. It happened the other day—I found out that my son and daughter-in-law are expecting another baby and I couldn't wait to tell Ron. I automatically went in and started to dial 1-8-4-7...then I said to myself, "What are you doing? Ron's not there. You can't talk to him. He's gone forever."

I've never been touched so deeply by anyone in my life as this man touched me in my heart—from how good he was to me, to my boys and in every situation that ever came up. I would have done anything in the world for him and his family. I truly would.

—**LINDA DILLMAN**, Bernie's Tavern Owner; Friend For 50 Years

In December, 2010, Vicki called me one morning and told me Ron was in bad shape and might not make it through the day and asked if I could help her with funeral arrangements. I told her I would do anything and everything she would need. That night, I had dinner with my son, who lives near Wrigley Field. I get a call from Vicki that Ron was not going to make it through the night. I pulled across the street with my son, Michael, and pulled into the Wrigley Field parking lot, which I hadn't done since I left the Cubs, and we said a prayer. I'm not a big religious guy, but I knew that night he was going to pass away. I'll remember that moment forever.

—**JOHN McDONOUGH**, Chicago Blackhawks President

The thing about the funeral that was most memorable for me was toward the end of the night, probably around 9:15—we'd been there for about eight hours plus—there was a twenty-year-old kid—a college student. He was standing in the back by himself and I walked up and introduced myself. I said, "Are you a big baseball fan?" He said, "No, I'm not really a Cubs fan." I said, "Interesting. So did you just like listening to Ron on the radio?" He said, "I don't really listen to the games. I'm not a baseball fan." Here was a kid who was a college student who took hours out of his evening to come to a wake for a guy he never met. So I said, "If you don't mind me asking, why are you here?" Here's a twenty-year-old kid who says, "I have Type I diabetes and Ron Santo raised sixty million dollars to help me and people like me. He didn't have to. No one else did. He's my hero."

—**TOM RICKETTS**, Cubs Chairman

He told me before he died—"Honey, I've had a great life. I was able to get up and be able to do what I loved to do and be able to provide for you kids. I've had a really good life." I would say to him, "You will be celebrated where you're going because you've fulfilled faith, hope, charity and love. I hope you have faith knowing that you're going to be okay because you've lived a wonderful life and you were good. And, you gave." He said he knew that. I told him, "I have peace knowing that you're going to a place where you've got some power to still take care of us." He was always thinking of his family. I knew this would still be important to him.

After the funeral service, we as a family drove in a motorcade behind my dad's hearse. We left Holy Name Cathedral and went down Michigan Avenue and looped around up to Wrigley Field. It was an amazing experience—the turnout of people just to pay their respects. I said to my boys, "No photo will ever capture this moment. Take this in right now. Take this in—all these fans. They're just gathering to see Grandpa's hearse—his casket." After that we parted ways at the I-90. The hearse went on to the Kennedy to go up north to the funeral home. Our three cars were going to Harry Caray's for the reception. It was our final parting, so to speak. He used to call me all the time on the way home from the games on this same route up north and report all the play-by-play details...it was his own 10th inning. This was his final drive up the Kennedy. I pictured him calling us one last time and recapping the beautiful service, how grateful he was to the Cubs for all they did to honor him and all the friends and fans who showed up saying, "Honey, it's Dad... did you see that? You would not believe the motorcade, all the fans! They came out of office buildings. They were taking pictures with their cell phones! They came out of bars and raised a beer. They were mobbing the car around Wrigley. It was unbelievable. They closed down Michigan Avenue...all for me!...can you believe that...?" and I would've answered "Yeah, I can believe that, Dad."

—**LINDA SANTO BROWN**

TO BE CONTINUED!

We hope you have enjoyed *Ron Santo: A Perfect 10*. Due to space and time considerations over 20 people with wonderful stories did not make the book, including teammates like Ernie Banks, Randy Hundley, Glenn Beckert, Ferguson Jenkins, and Don Kessinger.

Their stories will be included in *For Cub Fans Only, Volume III*. If you have a neat Ron Santo story or just an interesting Cubs story in general, contact us by e-mail at printedpage@cox. net (please put CUB FANS in the subject line and be sure to include a phone number where you can be reached), or call the author directly at (602) 738-5889.

Ditto for our upcoming books on the Bears and Notre Dame.

Note: No actual St. Louis Cardinals fans were harmed in the making of this book.

OTHER BOOKS BY RICH WOLFE

For Cubs Fans Only
For Cubs Fans Only—Volume II
For Notre Dame Fans Only—
   The New Saturday Bible
I Remember Harry Caray
Da Coach (Mike Ditka)
Tim Russert, We Heartily Knew Ye
For Packers Fans Only
For Hawkeye Fans Only
I Love It, I Love It, I Love It (with Jim Zabel, Iowa announcer)
Oh, What a Knight (Bob Knight)
There's No Expiration Date on Dreams (Tom Brady)
He Graduated Life with Honors and No Regrets (Pat Tillman)
Take This Job and Love It (Jon Gruden)
For Michigan Fans Only
For Milwaukee Braves Fans Only
Remembering Harry Kalas
Been There, Shoulda Done That (John Daly)
And the Last Shall Be First (Kurt Warner)
Remembering Jack Buck
Sports Fans Who Made Headlines
Fandemonium
Remembering Dale Earnhardt
I Saw It On the Radio (Vin Scully)
The Real McCoy (Al McCoy, Phoenix Suns announcer)
Personal Foul (With Tim Donaghy, former NBA referee)

For Yankee Fans Only	*For South Carolina Fans Only*
For Red Sox Fans Only	*For Clemson Fans Only*
For Cardinals Fans Only	*For Oklahoma Fans Only*
For Browns Fans Only	*For Yankee Fans Only—Volume II*
For Mets Fans Only	*For Mizzou Fans Only*
For Bronco Fans Only	*For Kansas City Chiefs Fans Only*
For Nebraska Fans Only	*For K-State Fans Only*
For Buckeye Fans Only	*For KU Fans Only (Kansas)*
For Georgia Bulldog Fans Only	*For Phillies Fans Only*

All books are the same size, format and price.
Questions or to order? Contact the author directly at 602-738-5889.